Mei Slow Cooker Book

Crock Pot Diet Cookbook with the Best Mediterranean Recipes for Beginners

(+ Healthy and Easy 7-Days Mediterranean Diet Plan for Weight Loss)

By

Helena Walker

Copyright [Helena Walker]

All rights reserved. No part of this guide may be reproduced in any form without permission in writing from the publisher except in the case of brief quotations embodied in critical articles or reviews.

Table of Contents

---❧---

*(MD) – means a perfect Mediterranean Diet recipe

Introduction 1
About the Mediterranean Diet 3
Crock Pot/Slow Cooker 7
Breakfast 10
    1. Mediterranean Crockpot Breakfast 10
    2. Slow Cooker Mediterranean Potatoes (MD) 13
    3. Mediterranean Crockpot Breakfast 15
    4. Mediterranean Crockpot Quiche 17
    5. Slow Cooker Mediterranean Meatloaf 19
    6. Slow Cooker Mediterranean Frittata (MD) 21
    7. Crock Pot Chicken Noodle Soup (MD) 23
    8. Hash Brown & Cheddar Breakfast 25
    9. Slow Cooker Fava Beans 27
    10. Pork Sausage Breakfast 30

Appetizers and Snacks 32
    1. Slow Cooker Crustless Mediterranean Quiche 32

2. Slow-Cooked Mediterranean Eggplant Salad (MD) 34

3. Crock Pot Mediterranean Meat Balls 36

4. Crock Pot Pizza Dip 39

5. Slow Cooker Mediterranean Mushroom (MD) 41

6. Slow Cooker Buffalo Meat Balls (MD) 43

7. Mediterranean Lentil & Chickpeas Appetizer (MD) 45

8. Yam & Red Bean Stew Mediterranean Style (MD) 48

9. Crock Pot Mediterranean Lentil Stew (MD) 50

10. Crock Pot Mediterranean Chickpeas Stew (MD) 53

Vegetables 55

1. Crock Pot Mediterranean Rice & Vegetables (MD) 55

2. Slow Cooker Spanish Chickpeas (MD) 57

3. Mediterranean Vegetable Curry (MD) 59

4. Italian Crock Pot Vegetable Dish (MD) 62

5. Mediterranean Vegetable Lasagna (MD) 64

6. Crock Pot Tortellini Stew (MD) 66

7. Slow Cooker Spinach Lasagna (MD) 68

8. Crock Pot Mediterranean Egg Plant Dish (MD) 70

9. Slow Cooker Ratatouille (MD) 72

10. Slow Cooker Beans Chili (MD) 74

Soup 76

1. Slow Cooker Lentil & Ham Soup 76

    2. Beef Barley Vegetable Soup 78

    3. Slow Cooker Corn Chowder 80

    4. Slow Cooker Chicken Posole (MD) 82

    5. Crock Pot Butternut Squash Soup (MD) 84

    6. Slow Cooker Mediterranean Chicken Soup (MD) 86

    7. Slow Cooker Chicken & Vegetable Soup (MD) 89

    8. Crock Pot Mediterranean Beef Soup 91

    9. Slow Cooker Split Pea Soup 93

    10. Slow Cooker Fish Soup (MD) 95

Pizza & Pasta **97**

    1. Crock Pot Pizza and Pasta 97

    2. Slow Cooker Beef Pizza 100

    3. Slow Cooker Deep Dish Pizza 102

    4. Mediterranean-Italian Style Pork Pizza 104

    5. Slow Cooker Mediterranean Pasta (MD) 106

    6. Slow Cooker Chicken Parmesan Pasta (MD) 108

    7. Slow Cooker Pasta Meat Sauce with Ground Turkey (MD) 110

    8. Crock Pot Pizza Casserole 113

    9. Slow Cooker Mediterranean Pasta 115

    10. Robust Mediterranean Sausage & Pasta 117

Beans & Grain **119**

~ v ~

1. Three Bean Mediterranean Slow Cooker Chili (MD) 119

2. Beans and Barley Stew (MD) 122

3. Mediterranean Lentils and Rice (MD) 124

4. Italian-Mediterranean Multi-Bean Soup(MD) 126

5. Mediterranean Slow Cooked Green Beans (MD) 128

6. Slow Cooked Green Beans 130

7. Slow Cooker Moroccan Chickpea Stew (MD) 132

8. Slow Cooker Spanish Rice (MD) 134

9. Slow Cooker Turkish/Mediterranean Chickpea Stew (MD) 136

10. Whole Wheat Crock Pot Lasagna (MD) 139

Chicken 141

1. Slow Cooker Mediterranean Chicken (MD) 141

2. Slow Cooker Greek Chicken (MD) 143

3. Crock Pot Mediterranean Chicken (MD) 145

4. Crock Pot Italian Chicken (MD) 147

5. Slow Cooker Italian Chicken (MD) 149

6. Crock Pot Greek Chicken & Salad (MD) 151

7. Slow Cooker Greek Chicken (MD) 153

8. Crock Pot Turkish Chicken (MD) 155

9. Slow Cooker Mediterranean Chicken & Chickpea Soup (MD) 157

10. Basque Chicken Stew (MD) 160

Meat 162

1. Slow Cooker Mediterranean Beef Roast 162
2. Slow Cooker Mediterranean Beef with Artichokes 164
3. Slow Cooker Mediterranean Beef Stew 166
4. Skinny Slow Cooker Mediterranean Style Pot Roast 168
5. Slow Cooker Meatloaf Recipe 170
6. Slow Cooker Mediterranean Beef Hoagies 173
7. Mediterranean Pork Roast 176
8. Pulled Pork with Bourbon-Peach Barbecue Sauce 178
9. Beef Stew with Rosemary & Balsamic Vinegar 181
10. Plum Pork Tenderloin 184

Fish & Seafood 186

1. Slow Cooker Mediterranean Salmon (MD) 186
2. Mediterranean Shrimp Soup (MD) 189
3. Slow Cooker Seafood Stew (MD) 191
4. Slow Cooker Spanish Shrimp Stew (MD) 193
5. Crock Pot Seafood Stew (MD) 195
6. Slow Cooker Salmon Risotto (MD) 197
7. Slow Cooker Mediterranean Shrimp Soup (MD) 199
8. Hearty Crock Pot Shrimp Stew (MD) 201
9. Mediterranean Cod with Pepper & Tomato (MD) 203

10. Mediterranean Seafood Stew (MD) 205

Mediterranean Desserts 207

1. Mediterranean Slow Cooker Apple Olive Cake (MD) 207

2. Mediterranean Crockpot Strawberry Basil Cobbler (MD) 210

3. Slow Cooker Mediterranean Pumpkin Pecan Bread Pudding 212

4. Slow Cooker Chocolate Fondue 214

5. Chocolate Orange Volcano Pudding 216

6. Slow Cooker Nutella Fudge 219

7. Greek Yogurt Chocolate Mousse (MD) 221

8. Peanut Butter Banana Greek Yogurt Bowl (MD) 223

9. Italian Slow Cooker Banana Foster 225

10. Mediterranean Rice Pudding 227

Meal Plan 229

7-Day Mediterranean Meal Plan 229

Conclusion 232

INTRODUCTION

The delightful flavors and delicious recipes of the Mediterranean diets prepared in a Crock Pot/Slow cooker are super yummy and luscious. I have been into the Mediterranean diet lately, and the recipes are irrefutably amazing. The recipes demand less time for preparation and are no-fuss cooking. All the ingredients are locally available, not limited to Mediterranean areas, and can be used for many other recipes.

It will be a new experience for people, who are under the illusion that making delicious Mediterranean appetizers, breakfast and soup recipes are not an easy business. The mouth-watering recipes are very easy to make and are wholesome as well.

This edition of the e-book deals with breakfasts, appetizers and snacks, vegetables, soups, pasta, pizzas, beans, grains, poultry, meat, fish, seafood, and deserts. The recipes have been developed to cater to the requirements of diverse tastes.

To tantalize your taste buds you should try the Pasta and Pizzas recipes in this book. The delectable dishes will grab your interest and attention.

Cooking is a wonderful and enjoyable experience, and you should enjoy every bit of it. Ingredients where fish, seafood, and beans have been used in recipes can be substituted with any locally available items, if some are not available in your kitchen or

Henry Wilson

groceries. You will have such an easy breezy day with tasty Mediterranean recipes of poultry and soup which are perfect for dinner or any other meals in the day.

In Mediterranean diets, fish recipes have a predominant position, and you can find ten delectable seafood recipes in this e-book. You can never go wrong with the easygoing and effortless recipes of this book. The flavorsome and ambrosial dessert recipes are tasty and satisfying. The recipes will ensure clean plates, and they'll become your go-to food.

Cooking these delectable dishes in a slow cooker or crockpot is more fun because you are going to enjoy every bit of each step. Garnish the mouth-watering recipes of the Mediterranean diet with spring onions or herbs. Basil leaves also provide a fantastic flavor to your dish.

Get your sunny day started with the best Mediterranean dishes in this book. People always say that good food makes you think well in life and that's why we have this incredible book right here for you.

Enjoy every bit of your life with the delectable Mediterranean recipes!

About the Mediterranean Diet

Apart from being a foodie, it is essential to maintain a good and balanced diet. Staying fit and healthy should be the primary goal of every individual irrespective of the food habit. The Mediterranean diet revolves around the concept of healthy eating, and the recipes lavishly use olive oil and sometimes a few ounces of red wine, which are the inevitable traditional cooking ingredients. The Mediterranean diet reflects the various conventional cooking style in practice bordering the Mediterranean Sea and surrounding areas.

The diet comprises of fish, meat and vegetables and a few spices. Apart from these points the menu also includes fruits along with olive oil, whole grains, and beans. Some compromises are also made regarding dairy food. The entire diet if observed from the fitness point of view has many more inclusions. These recipes are not like a typical diet which restricts you to eat a specific food. The diet aims to feed nutritious and tasty food to everyone, along with some weight loss benefits.

The Mediterranean diet is effective in terms of eating healthy and losing weight. The food also prevents many diseases like heart attacks, strokes, untimely death, and diabetes. If anyone is on a Mediterranean diet, then it is significant to follow the underlying philosophies and rudiments of this diet. Some of the diet principles are as follow:–

Mediterranean diet facts:

- Using lots of herbs and less salt to maintain the flavor.
- Concentrate on vegetables, fruits, nuts, whole grains, legumes, etc.
- Consume fish or seafood at least twice a week.
- Vegetables such as broccoli, tomato, spinach, sprouts, onion, cauliflower, and Brussels must be added in the diet daily.
- Walnuts, hazelnuts, almonds, pumpkin seeds and cashews should also be consumed if you are on a Mediterranean diet.
- Fish and kinds of seafood such as tuna, sardines, trout, mackerel, shrimp, mussels, clams, oysters, crab, etc., must be included in the diet.
- Dairy, poultry, and eggs are a necessity of a Mediterranean diet, and hence they should be added as well.
- Avoid or restrict the use of red meat to the minimum possible.
- Extra virgin olive oil and avocado oil along with olives and avocados must also be added in the diet to make it healthy and nutritious.
- If we move on towards drinks, water is an integral part of the Mediterranean diet. Water should be consumed whenever you feel like drinking anything else.
- Some red wine is also acceptable in this diet.

- Limited intake of tea and coffee are acceptable but avoid sugar-sweetened and carbonated beverages.

Foods to avoid

The list of principles also includes some unwholesome foods which you should avoid during the Mediterranean diet.

- Processed meat like hot dogs and processed sausages should be avoided on this diet.
- Sugary drinks and desserts like ice-cream, candies, soda and many more should also be avoided.
- Refined oils like soybean oil, cottonseed oil, and canola oil should be avoided.
- White bread and whole wheat pasta (pasta made from refined wheat) should avoid during the entire diet plan.

The Mediterranean diet is a combination of eating healthy food and avoiding large quantities of food. Fruits, rice, vegetables, and pasta are significant in the Mediterranean diet. Wholegrain bread is an essential item in the Mediterranean diet. Nuts are another item which are commonly used in the Mediterranean diet. Though nuts are high in fat, it does not contain saturated fat; however, we recommend limiting the consumption of nuts in a day, to not more than a handful.

The Mediterranean diet plan restricts the use of hydrogenated oil and saturated fats, which are the reason for heart diseases. You can find a moderate quantity of virgin or extra virgin olive oils are used in Mediterranean recipes because these are the lowest form of processed oils and contains lots of antioxidants.

What should be your food choice?

- Eat lots of fruits and vegetables.
- Consume wholegrain bread or cereal, wholegrain rice or pasta items.
- Enjoy nuts, but avoid roasted and salted.
- Replace butter with canola or olive oil.
- Consume fish twice a week, especially salmon, tuna, mackerel, herring, trout, etc. Limit the consumption of fried fish.
- Limit the consumption of red meat. It would be better if you can substitute it with poultry or seafood items. Say no to red meat sausages, bacon, etc.
- Include more herbs and spices. It can improve your metabolism and digestion process.
- Make it a practice to consume low-fat dairy products, such as skimmed milk, low-fat cheese, no-fat yogurt, etc.

The Mediterranean diet plan tackles possible heart-health issues, and it derived the food habits of people living in the Mediterranean Sea area. People living in these areas are comparatively healthy than those people living in other parts of the world. We can find many research studies on this subject, backing the benefits of the Mediterranean diet, which helps to prevent heart ailments, promote weight loss, prevent strokes, type 2 diabetes, etc.

This e-book engages with various Mediterranean diets, based upon the food habits prevailing in and around Mediterranean countries. Since there are many cooking styles available, you have the liberty to select the recipe that meets your preferences.

Crock Pot/Slow Cooker

Why A Crock Pot/Slow Cooker Is The Best To Use For Mediterranean Diet Meals?

Famous as the world's healthiest diet, the Mediterranean diet is renowned for its impressive roster of health rewards including weight reduction, heart protection, and cancer prevention. The diet is abundant in vegetables, fruits, legumes, whole grains, and olive oil and features both poultry and fish over red meat.

With the ability to cook hearty stews and fall off the bone braises with little or no supervision, crock pots are the best to use for Mediterranean diet meals. Who wouldn't love lean meat and vegetables slow cooked in its juices alone? The Mediterranean diet isn't a strict diet plan; it just mimics the healthy way of eating followed by people in Mediterranean countries for centuries. Now you know why both the crockpot and the Mediterranean diet make a great combination.

Here is how to make the most of your Mediterranean diet

Make vegetables a significant part of your meal

Vegetables and fruits must make up the bulk of your meals. You can have up to 7 servings of vegetables and fruits a day, and it will show a significant difference in reducing the risk of heart diseases. When you are on a Mediterranean diet, wire your brain to think of all possible ways to add more vegetables to your meals like adding cucumber, avocado and olive oil to your salads, or adding spinach to eggs or swapping your evening snacks with fruits.

Say no to red meat

Lean protein like chicken or fatty fish like tuna, salmon, etc., are the primary protein sources you need to include in the diet. Choose fish which contains high doses of omega 3 fatty acids which contain several health benefits. Swap red meat for good lean protein sources, you can have red meat in limited quantity and frequency along with cheese and yogurt.

Cook with olive oil

As you will see, most of the recipes I have created use olive oil instead of butter or any other oils. The Mediterranean diet focuses on eating more healthy fats and few trans fats or saturated fats. Swap up butter for olive oil to lower cholesterol levels and improve your heart health.

Skip the sugar, all the time

Avoid eating sugar, especially white sugar. Do not munch on crackers, processed cookies, refined flours as these are strictly not a part of the Mediterranean diet. Save ice-creams and sweats for special occasions and never eat them often. Instead of refined sugar, pick fresh fruits or nuts like dates and figs to satisfy your sweet tooth.

Benefits of using a crock pot for your Mediterranean diet

- **Makes a meal at home an effortless task** – Crockpot allows one-step preparation, you need to place the ingredients in the cooker, and it does it all.
- **Saves preparation time** – You hardly need to do anything after placing all the ingredients. In the given time the meal ill be ready and you can invest your time in other chores. It also cuts down on the cleaning process as the food is prepared in a single pot.
- **Brings out the flavor in food** - As the Mediterranean diet consists of all healthy ingredients, that are flavorful, the slow cooking method brings the best taste in foods.
- **Uses less electricity** - It would be so nice to save some energy bills too while cooking your favorite meal. Compared to the oven or any other electrical appliances, slow cookers uses less electricity.

BREAKFAST

---

1. Mediterranean Crockpot Breakfast

Preparation: 15 minutes | Cooking: 7 hours | Servings: 8

Ingredients:

- Eggs - 1 dozen

- Hash brown potatoes - 2 pounds
- Milk - 1 cup
- Shredded cheddar cheese - 3 cups
- Diced onions - ½ cup
- Bacon – 1 pound
- Garlic powder - ¼ teaspoon
- Dry mustard - ¼ teaspoon
- Salt - 1 teaspoon
- Pepper - ½ teaspoon
- Spring onions – for garnishing

Cooking directions:

1. Beat the eggs using a blender until they gets combined well with one another
2. Now add garlic powder, milk, salt, mustard, and pepper along with the beaten eggs and continue blending. Keep aside.
3. Season the hash brown potatoes with pepper and salt.
4. Place the hash brown potatoes in layer by layer and diced onions into the crockpot.
5. Sprinkle a quarter portion of bacon and mix them well together
6. Add a cup of cheese to the crockpot to make it a smooth looking texture.
7. Repeat this layering process two to three times
8. Now pour the blended egg mixture over the layers of hash potatoes in the crockpot.
9. Set slow cooking for 7 hours.
10. Garnish with finely chopped spring onions while serving.

Henry Wilson

Nutritional values:

Calories: 416 | Carbohydrate: 23g | Protein: 29g | Sugars: 2g |Fat: 33g | Dietary Fiber: 1g | Cholesterol: 294mg | Sodium: 766mg

Mediterranean Diet Slow Cooker Book

2. Slow Cooker Mediterranean Potatoes

(Perfect Mediterranean Diet recipe)

Preparation: 5 minutes | Cooking: 5 hours | Servings: 8

Ingredients:

- Fingerling potatoes - 3 pounds
- Dried oregano - 1 tablespoon
- Olive oil - 2 tablespoons
- Smoked paprika - 1 teaspoon
- Unsalted butter - 2 tablespoons
- Ground black pepper, fresh – 1 teaspoon
- Lemon juice - 1 teaspoon
- Minced garlic - 4 cloves
- Fresh parsley leaves, chopped - 2 tablespoons

- Kosher salt - ½ teaspoon
- Lemon - 1 zest

Cooking directions:

1. Peel, wash potatoes and cut into half. Keep aside.
2. Slightly grease the inside of a 6-quart slow cooker with non-stick spray.
3. Add olive oil, potatoes, lemon juice, butter, paprika, and oregano in the cooker
4. Season by using pepper and salt
5. Close the lid.
6. Set it to slow cook for 5 hours.
7. Serve hot by garnishing with chopped parsley and lemon zest.

Nutritional values:

Calories: 179.5 | Carbohydrate: 28.4g | Protein: 3.1g | Sugars: 2.2g | Fat: 6.5g | Dietary Fiber: 4.6g | Cholesterol: 7.6mg | Sodium: 11.8mg

3. Mediterranean Crockpot Breakfast

Preparation: 15 minutes | Cooking: 4 hours | Servings: 8

Ingredients:

- Hash browns, frozen - 30 ounces
- Eggs - 8
- Milk - ¾ cup
- Egg whites - 4
- Garlic salt - ½ teaspoon
- Ground mustard – 2 teaspoon
- Cooked bacon - 4 strips
- Roughly chopped bell peppers - 2
- Onion chopped coarsely - ½
- Cheddar cheese - 6 ounces

- Roughly chopped broccoli head - 1 small
- Pepper - ½ teaspoon
- Salt - 1 teaspoon

Cooking directions:

1. Whisk eggs, milk, egg whites, garlic salt, mustard, pepper, and salt together in a medium bowl and keep aside.
2. Slightly grease the bottom of the crockpot.
3. Add half of the hash browns into the crockpot and set it as the bottom layer.
4. Over this layer of hash browns, put chopped onion, bacon, broccoli, bell peppers and cheese.
5. Now, add the remaining hash browns and make a new layer
6. Top this second layer with the remaining bacon, vegetables, and cheese.
7. Pour the egg mixture on top of these layers.
8. Cover the crockpot and slow cook for four hours.
9. Serve hot.

Nutritional values:

Calories: 320 | Carbohydrate: 29g | Protein: 22g | Sugars: 1g | Fat: 13g | Dietary Fiber: 5g | Cholesterol: 215mg | Sodium: 700mg

4. Mediterranean Crockpot Quiche

Preparation: 15 minutes | Cooking: 6-hour | Servings: 9

Ingredients:

- Milk – 1 cup
- Eggs – 8
- Feta cheese, crumbled - 1½ cup
- Bisquick mix – 1 cup
- Spinach, fresh, chopped – 2 cups
- Red bell pepper - ½ cup
- Garlic, nicely chopped – 1 teaspoon
- Basil leaves, fresh - ¼ cup
- Sausage crumbles fully cooked – 9.6 ounces
- Feta cheese, crumbled (for garnishing) - ¼ cup

Henry Wilson

Cooking directions:

1. Grease a 5-quart slow cooker with cooking spray.
2. In a large bowl, whisk eggs, Bisquick mix, milk thoroughly.
3. Add one, and half crumbled feta cheese, garlic, basil, sausage, bell pepper and stir the entire mix thoroughly.
4. Close the lid and set slow cooking for 6 hours.
5. Your Quiche will be ready when the center becomes firm and sides become golden brown.
6. Cut into pieces for serving.
7. Garnish with feta cheese sprinkling.

Nutritional values:

Calories: 308 | Carbohydrate: 13.7g | Protein: 17g | Sugars: 3.7g | Fat: 21g | Dietary Fiber: 0.3g | Cholesterol: 191mg | Sodium: 928mg | Potassium: 241mg

5. Slow Cooker Mediterranean Meatloaf

Preparation: 15 minutes | Cooking: 4 hours | Servings: 4

Ingredients:

- Minced Beef - ½ pound
- Tomato sauce – 2 cups
- Onion, diced - 1 small
- Bacon unsmoked - 4
- Red wine - ½ cup
- Mustard - 1 teaspoon
- Cheddar cheese - 1 Oz
- Oregano - 1 teaspoon
- Garlic puree - 1 teaspoon
- Thyme - 1 teaspoon
- Paprika - 1 teaspoon

- Salt - ½ teaspoon
- Pepper - ½ teaspoon
- Parsley - 1 teaspoon
- Fresh herbs – as required

Cooking directions:

1. In a large bowl put all the seasoning items.
2. Add onion and minced beef to the bowl and mix well by combing with your hands.
3. Spread the mixture on a clean worktop and press it forms like a pastry, which can roll out cleanly.
4. In the middle portion of the meatloaf pastry, layer some chopped cheese.
5. After adding the cheese as a layer, wrap the meat like a sausage roll.
6. Pour little olive oil into the slow cooker for greasing and then place the roll.
7. Mix homemade tomato sauce and red wine in a separate bowl and pour it on the sides of the meatloaf.
8. Do not pour this mixture over the meatloaf
9. Now, spread the bacon over the meatloaf.
10. Slow cook it for four hours.
11. Serve hot along with roast vegetables and potatoes.

Nutritional values:

Calories: 385 | Carbohydrate: 14g | Protein: 17g | Sugars: 8g | Fat: 26g | Dietary Fiber: 3g | Cholesterol: 66mg | Sodium: 603mg |Potassium: 597mg

6. Slow Cooker Mediterranean Frittata

(Perfect Mediterranean Diet recipe)

Preparation: 30 minutes | Cooking: 3 hours | Servings: 6

Ingredients:

- Eggs - 8
- Oregano, dried - 1 teaspoon
- Milk - ⅓ cup
- Red peppers, chopped and roasted - 1¼ cup
- Baby arugula - 4 cups
- Ground pepper, fresh - ½ teaspoon
- Goats' cheese, grated - ¾ cup
- Red onion, finely sliced - ½ cup

- Salt - ½ teaspoon

Cooking directions:

1. Spray some non-stick oil into the slow cooker.
2. In a large bowl whisk milk, eggs, and oregano together.
3. Season it with salt and pepper as per your taste.
4. Arrange the roasted red pepper, baby arugula, goat cheese and red onion in the slow cooker
5. Pour the egg mixture over the vegetables.
6. Let it slow cook for 3 hours.
7. Serve hot.

Nutritional values:

Calories: 164 | Carbohydrate: 4g | Protein: 17g | Sugars: 3g | Fat: 11g

7. Crock Pot Chicken Noodle Soup

(Perfect Mediterranean Diet recipe)

Preparation: 15 minutes | Cooking: 6 hours 10 minutes | Servings: 4

Ingredients:

- Chicken breasts, boneless and skinless, cut into ½" size – 3
- Chicken broth - 5½ cup
- Chopped celery stalks - 3
- Chopped carrots - 3
- Chopped onion - 1

- Bay leaf - 1
- Minced garlic cloves - 3
- Peas, frozen - 1 cup
- Egg noodles - 2½ cup
- Fresh parsley, chopped - ¼ cup
- Ground black pepper, fresh - ½ teaspoon
- Salt - ½ teaspoon

Cooking directions:

1. Place chicken breasts in the bottom of the slow cooker.
2. On top of the chicken put onion, celery stalks, garlic cloves, and carrots.
3. Pour in the chicken broth and put the bay leaf in.
4. Add pepper and salt as per your taste.
5. Cook on slow cook mode for 6 hours.
6. After six hours, add egg noodles and frozen peas to the cooker
7. Cook further about 5-6 minutes until the egg noodles turn tender.
8. Stir in chopped fresh parsley
9. Serve hot.

Nutritional values:

Calories: 527 | Carbohydrate: 44g | Protein: 61g | Sugars: 11g

8. Hash Brown & Cheddar Breakfast

Preparation: 30 minutes | Cooking: 6 hours | Servings: 12

Ingredients:

- Hash browns, frozen & shredded - 32 ounces
- Onion, green, coarsely chopped - 6
- Breakfast sausage, crumbled & cooked - 16 ounces
- Eggs - 12
- Shredded cheddar cheese - 12 ounces
- Garlic powder - ¼ teaspoon
- Milk - ¼ cup
- Pepper - ½ teaspoon
- Salt - 1 teaspoon

- Pepper – 1 teaspoon for seasoning.
- Salt - ½ teaspoon for seasoning.

Cooking directions:

1. Oil a 6-quart slow cooker with non-stick cooking spray.
2. In the slow cooker, layer ⅓ portion of hash brown.
3. Season this layer with pepper and salt.
4. Now, layer ⅓ portion of the cooked and crumbled sausage over the first layer.
5. Again layer ⅓ portion of both cheddar cheese and green onions over the sausage.
6. Repeat both these layers twice, ending with cheese
7. Take a large bowl and whisk milk, egg, salt, garlic powder and pepper together.
8. Pour this egg mixture all over the sausage, hash brown and cheese layers in the slow cooker.
9. Slow cook it for about six to eight hours until the edges turn brown and the center become firm.
10. Serve hot.

Nutritional values:

Calories: 431 | Carbohydrate: 17g | Protein: 24g | Fat: 29g | Dietary Fiber: 1g | Cholesterol: 265mg | Sodium: 831mg | Potassium: 505mg

9. Slow Cooker Fava Beans

Preparation: 10 minutes | Cooking: 8 hours | Servings: 12

Ingredients:

- Fava beans (dried) - 1 pound
- Red lentils – 3 tablespoons
- Uncooked rice – 3 tablespoons
- Tomato, chopped - 1
- Garlic, chopped – 3 cloves
- Water – as required (about 2 cups)
- Salt - ½ teaspoon

For sausage:

- Onion, finely sliced in rings - ½
- Tomato – 1 small
- Olive oil – 2 tablespoons

Henry Wilson

- Sausages, cut into halves – 4
- Cumin seed - ¼ teaspoon
- Lemon juice - ½ teaspoon

Cooking directions:

1. Soak the fava beans for about 4 hours.
2. Wash and drain the beans.
3. Put the drained beans in a 6-quart slow cooker.
4. Wash the lentils, rice, and drain.
5. Put the drained lentils and rice also into the slow cooker.
6. Now add the chopped tomato and garlic into the slow cooker.
7. Add water above the ingredients level.
8. Set the slow cooking for 8 hours.
9. When cooking over, prepare the sausages.
10. Pour olive oil in non-stick pan and bring to heat at a medium-high temperature.
11. When the oil becomes hot, add chopped onions and sauté on medium heat until it becomes tender.
12. Now add chopped garlic and continue stirring until the fragrance starts to release.
13. Add cumin seeds and continue stirring.
14. After that add chopped tomatoes and sausages.
15. Continue stirring for 5 minutes.
16. Now transfer the cooked beans over the sausages.
17. Drizzle the lemon juice over the beans.
18. Add salt if required.
19. Stir the mix and cook for 2-3 minutes to warm the food.
20. Serve hot.

Nutritional values:

Calories: 99.9 | Carbohydrate: 19g | Protein: 7.1g | Sodium: 4.3g | Fat: 0.5g | Dietary Fiber: 7.2g

10. Pork Sausage Breakfast

Preparation: 15 minutes | Cooking: 6 hours 05 minutes | Servings: 12

Ingredients:

- Pork sausage - 16 ounce
- Eggs - 12
- Milk - 1 cup
- Veg oil – 2 tablespoons
- Hash brown potatoes, frozen - 26 ounces
- Ground mustard - 1 tablespoon
- Ground black pepper - as per taste required
- Cheddar cheese, shredded - 16 ounces.
- Salt - ½ teaspoon

- Pepper - ¾ teaspoon
- Cooking spray – as required

Cooking directions:

1. Spray some non-stick cooking oil into the bottom of your crockpot.
2. Layer the hash brown potatoes in the crockpot.
3. Now pour vegetable oil into a large skillet and heat on medium high temperature.
4. When the oil becomes hot put the sausages in, stir and continue cooking for 7 minutes until it becomes brown and crumbly.
5. Once the cooking is over, remove the sausage and discard the oil.
6. Now, spread the sausage over the hash brown potatoes and top it with cheddar cheese.
7. Beat milk and eggs together in a separate large bowl.
8. Add ground mustard along with salt and pepper to this mixture and stir thoroughly.
9. Pour this mixture on top of the cheese layer.
10. Set on slow cook for six hours. If you wish you can further slow down the cooking to 8 hours or even more time.
11. Serve hot.

Nutritional values:

Calories: 382 | Carbohydrate: 13.1g | Protein: 22.8g | Fat: 30g | Cholesterol: 248mg | Sodium: 680mg |Potassium: 508mg | Dietary Fiber: 0.9g | Sugars: 2g

APPETIZERS AND SNACKS

1. Slow Cooker Crustless Mediterranean Quiche

Preparation: 15 minutes | Cooking: 3 hours 15 minutes | Servings: 9

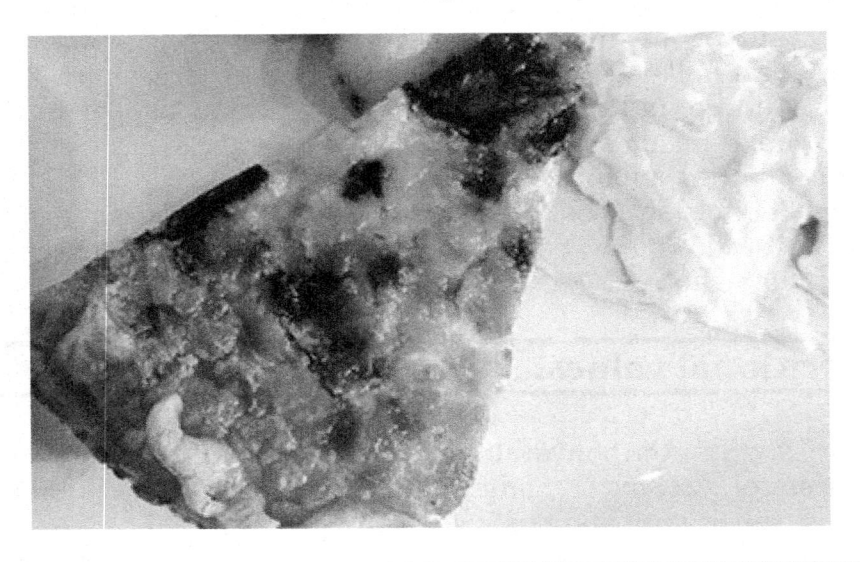

Ingredients:

- Milk - 1 cup

- Eggs - 8
- Fresh spinach fresh - 2 cups
- Bisquick mix - 1 cup
- Red bell peppers, roasted - ½ cup
- Feta cheese, grated - 6 ounces
- Garlic, finely chopped - 1 teaspoon
- Basil leaves, fresh, chopped - ¼ cup
- Sausage crumbles (cooked) - 9.6 ounces
- Feta cheese, grated (for garnish) - ¼ cup
- Non-stick cooking spray

Cooking directions:

1. Lightly grease a 5-quart slow cooker with non-stick cooking spray.
2. Whisk milk, eggs, and Bisquick mix until they get mixed well together in a medium bowl.
3. Pour this mix to the slow cooker.
4. Add feta cheese, spinach, basil, bell peppers, sausage, and garlic to the slow cooker and stir well.
5. Cover the cooker and slow cook for 6 hours.
6. Check the cooking status after 6 hours. If the center is firm, then it is ready to serve.
7. Cut and serve hot by sprinkling feta cheese.

Nutritional values:

Calories: 226 | Carbohydrate: 3.2g | Protein: 14.7g | Sugars: 2.7g |Fat: 17.1g | Dietary Fiber: 0.3g | Cholesterol: 190mg | Sodium: 510mg | Potassium: 220mg

2. Slow-Cooked Mediterranean Eggplant Salad

(Perfect Mediterranean Diet recipe)

Preparation: 15 minutes | Cooking: 8 hours | Servings: 6

Ingredients:

- Eggplant quartered sliced – 1 large
- Bell peppers, sliced - 2
- Red onion, sliced - 1
- Canned tomatoes - 24 ounces
- Cumin - 2 teaspoons
- Smoked paprika - 1 tablespoon

- Black pepper – 1 teaspoon
- Salt – ¾ teaspoon
- Lemon juice - 1 tablespoon

Cooking directions:

1. Put all ingredients in a slow cooker and combine.
2. Slow cook for eight hours.
3. Serve hot.

Nutritional values:

Calories: 67 | Carbohydrate: 14.8g | Protein: 2.7g | Sugars: 8.2g | Fat: 0.8g | Dietary Fiber: 5.6g | Cholesterol: 0mg | Sodium: 30mg | Potassium: 592mg

3. Crock Pot Mediterranean Meat Balls

Preparation: 20 minutes | Cooking: 4 hours | Servings: 25

Ingredients:

For meatballs:

- Minced onion - ¼ cup
- Meat (Ground Pork or beef) - 2 pounds
- Chopped fresh parsley - 3 tablespoons
- Minced garlic - 3 cloves
- Eggs - 2
- Breadcrumbs (seasoned) - 1 cup
- Ground pepper – 1 teaspoon
- Crumbled parmesan cheese - ¾ cup
- Salt - as required

For the sauce:

- Crushed tomatoes – 48 ounces
- Bay leaf - 1 whole
- Tomato paste - 6 ounces
- Italian seasoning - 1 teaspoon
- Red pepper flakes, crushed - ½ teaspoon
- Salt - as per taste required
- Pepper – 1 teaspoon
- Oregano - 1 teaspoon

Extra for garnishing

- Parmesan cheese, grated - ¼ cup
- Fresh parsley, chopped - ¼ cup.

Cooking directions:

1. In a large bowl mix onion, meat, breadcrumbs, cheese, parsley, salt, eggs, and pepper by hand.
2. Make meatballs with the mix. Keep the meatball size between 1 and 2 inches.
3. Take a baking sheet and lightly grease it
4. Broil the meatballs under high heat until the balls turn brown on both sides.
5. Make sure to turn the meatballs intermittently to have an even browning.
6. Once the meatballs turn golden brown, transfer it to the crockpot.
7. To prepare the sauce, take a new bowl and mix ingredients mentioned under the sauce category.
8. Pour this mix directly all over the meatballs.
9. Stir around the meatballs and make sure the balls coated thoroughly with the sauce.
10. Cook on low heat about 4 hours

11. Sprinkle grated parmesan cheese and chopped fresh parsley before serving.
12. Serve hot.

Nutritional values:

Calories: 148 | Carbohydrate: 6.9g | Protein: 11.2g |Fat: 8.3g | Dietary Fiber: 1.2g | Sodium: 77mg |Cholesterol: 47mg |Sugars: 2.6g | Potassium: 350mg

4. Crock Pot Pizza Dip

Preparation: 5 minutes | Cooking: 2 hours | Servings: 20

Ingredients:

- Italian seasoning - 1 teaspoon
- Soft cream cheese - 8 ounces
- Parmesan cheese, shredded - ¾ cup
- Mozzarella cheese, grated - 1 cup
- Pepperoni pieces, cut piece - 1/4 cup
- Pizza sauce - 8 ounces

Cooking directions:

1. In a crock pot put all the ingredients.
2. Set on high cooking for about 1 hour.
3. After an hour, when the cheese starts to melt, turn the setting to low and continue cooking for one more hour.
4. Serve hot.

Nutritional values:

Calories: 81 | Carbohydrate: 1g | Protein: 3g | Fat: 6g | Cholesterol: 21mg | Sodium: 213mg | Potassium: 66mg

5. Slow Cooker Mediterranean Mushroom

(Perfect Mediterranean Diet recipe)

Preparation: 10 minutes | Cooking: 3 hours | Servings: 6

Ingredients:

- Mushrooms (White button) - 16 ounces
- Fresh parsley, finely chopped - ¼ cup
- Virgin olive oil – 2 tablespoons
- Garlic, finely chopped – 3 cloves
- Black pepper - ¼ teaspoon
- Salt – 1 teaspoon

Cooking directions:

1. Wash, clean and pat dry mushrooms.
2. Cut off the ends and cut into quarters.
3. Pour olive oil into the slow cooker.
4. Now put all the ingredients in the slow cooker.
5. Slow cook for 3 hours.
6. Serve along with ketchup.

Nutritional values

Calories: 60 | Carbohydrate: 3.2g | Protein: 2.6g | Sugars: 1.3g |Fat: 4.9g | Dietary Fiber: 0.9g | Sodium: 394mg | Potassium: 261mg | Cholesterol: 0mg |Potassium: 261mg

6. Slow Cooker Buffalo Meat Balls

(Perfect Mediterranean Diet recipe)

Preparation: 20 minutes | Cooking: 3 hours 40 minutes | Servings: 6

Ingredients:

- Egg - 1 large
- Ground turkey - 1 pound
- Thinly sliced green onions - 3
- Onion powder - ½ teaspoon
- Garlic powder - ½ teaspoon
- Grounded black pepper, fresh - ½ teaspoon

- Kosher salt - ½ teaspoon
- Bread crumbs - ¾ cup
- Frank's Wing Sauce - ¾ cup
- Non-stick spray – as required
- Blue cheese for dressing - ¼ cup
- Scallions, chopped - ¼ cup

Cooking directions:

1. Preheat the oven at 200 degrees Celsius
2. Prepare a baking sheet by applying non-stick spray and set it aside.
3. Combine eggs, ground turkey, garlic, green onions and onion powder in a large bowl.
4. Add pepper, salt, panko and season it.
5. Stir all these ingredients either using a wooden spoon or hands
6. Roll the mixture into one, and a half inch sized meatballs
7. The mixture is enough to make 24 meatballs.
8. Now, place the meatballs into the already prepared baking sheet and bake it for 4-5 minutes until all sides become brown.
9. Now place the meatballs into the slow cooker.
10. Add buffalo sauce all over the meatballs and gently toss it.
11. Cover the cooker and slow cook for 2 hours.
12. Spread blue cheese before serving
13. Before serving the meatballs, drizzle some blue cheese all over them with chopped scallions.

Nutritional values:

Calories: 548 | Carbohydrate: 24g | Protein: 31g | Sugars: 4g |Fat: 36g | Dietary Fiber: 2g | Cholesterol: 176mg | Sodium: 825mg

7. Mediterranean Lentil & Chickpeas Appetizer

(Perfect Mediterranean Diet recipe)

Preparation: 15 minutes | Cooking: 8 hours | Servings: 8

Ingredients:

- Chickpeas, canned – 14 ounces
- Finely chopped sweet onion - 1
- Green lentils - 1½ cup
- Minced garlic - 2 cloves
- Grated fresh ginger - 1 inch
- Chopped red bell pepper - 1
- Chopped carrots - 3

- Chicken broth - 4 cups
- Diced tomatoes - 14 ounce
- Smoked paprika - 2 teaspoons
- Red harissa - 2 tablespoons
- Cinnamon - ¾ teaspoon
- Cumin - ¾ teaspoon
- Fresh lemon juice - 1 tablespoon
- Kosher salt - ½ teaspoon
- Pepper - ¾ teaspoon
- Cilantro, fresh chopped - ½ cup
- Water - ½ cup

For garnishing:

- Toasted almonds - ¼ cup
- Goat cheese, grated - ½ cup

Cooking directions:

1. In a crockpot, put onion, lentils, garlic, ginger, red pepper, carrots, chicken broth, tomatoes, harissa, half a cup of water, cumin, paprika, salt, pepper, and cinnamon.
2. Stir all these ingredients to combine thoroughly.
3. Cover and slow cook for 8 hours.
4. Before serving the soup, put chickpeas, lemon juice, and cilantro and cook until it simmers.
5. If the soup consistency is thick, add water or chicken broth.
6. Taste and adjust the salt levels are per your taste.
7. Garnish the soup with toasted almonds, grated goat cheese, and fresh cilantro.
8. Serve hot.

Nutritional values:

Calories: 251 | Carbohydrate: 39.2g | Protein: 13.7g | Sugars: 9.5g |Fat: 5.2g | Dietary Fiber: 10.9g | Cholesterol: 0mg | Sodium: 590mg | Potassium: 802mg

8. Yam & Red Bean Stew Mediterranean Style

(Perfect Mediterranean Diet recipe)

Preparation: 30 minutes | Cooking: 10 hours| Servings: 8

Ingredients:

- Yam, peeled and chopped – 2 pounds
- Onion, chopped - 1 large
- Dried red beans - ½ cup
- Minced garlic - 3 cloves
- Red bell peppers, chopped - 2 large
- Fresh ginger, minced - 2 tablespoons
- Vegetable stock - 3 cups
- Jalapeno pepper, minced - 3
- Diced large tomatoes - 14 ounces

- Ground cumin - ½ teaspoon
- Salt - ½ teaspoon
- Ground cinnamon - ¼ teaspoon
- Ground coriander - ½ teaspoon
- Creamy peanut butter - ¼ cup
- Ground black pepper - ¼ teaspoon
- Lime wedges - 1
- Dry roasted peanuts - ¼ cup

Cooking directions:

1. Soak the beans overnight.
2. In a crock pot, combine bell peppers, onion, ginger, garlic, stock, yams, jalapenos, tomatoes, cumin, salt, cinnamon, coriander, and black pepper.
3. Combine it thoroughly.
4. Later on, add the beans that have kept for soaking.
5. Stir before you start cooking it.
6. Cover the crockpot and cook for 10 hours. Before serving, make sure the beans and Yams have become tender.
7. Before serving the stew, mix peanut butter with a small portion of the stew in a different bowl. Combine it thoroughly.
8. Transfer the peanut butter mixture into the crock pot and stir with the stew.
9. Top the stew with dry roasted peanuts and squeeze fresh lemon juice before serving.

Nutritional values:

Calories: 200 | Carbohydrate: 44.6g | Protein: 5.3g | Fat: 0.5g | Dietary Fiber: 7.7g | Cholesterol: 0.0mg | Sodium: 175mg | Potassium: 1122mg | Sugars: 4.4g

9. Crock Pot Mediterranean Lentil Stew

(Perfect Mediterranean Diet recipe)

Preparation: 10 minutes | Cooking: 6 hours | Servings: 4

Ingredients:

- Vegetable broth - 7 cups
- Green lentils, dry - 2 cups
- Ground coriander - 1½ tablespoon
- Apple cider vinegar - 1 tablespoon
- Ground ginger - ½ teaspoon
- Ground cumin - 1½ teaspoon
- Ground cloves - ¼ teaspoon
- Ground cardamom - ⅛ teaspoon

- Ground nutmeg - ⅛ teaspoon
- Cinnamon stick - 1
- Ground cayenne pepper - ½ teaspoon
- Bay leaf - 1
- Smoked paprika - ½ teaspoon
- Salt - 1 teaspoon
- Chopped carrot - 1 large
- Minced garlic - 3 cloves
- Sweet potato - 2 cups

For seasoning:

- Plain yogurt - ½ cup
- Golden raisins - ¼ cup

Cooking directions:

1. Rinse the lentils under running tap water, dry and keep aside.
2. Put apple cider vinegar, vegetable broth, ground coriander, ground cumin, ground cardamom, ground ginger, cinnamon stick, ground cloves, ground cayenne pepper, ground nutmeg, bay leaf, smoked paprika, salt, garlic, carrot, and sweet potato into a crock pot.
3. Mix all these ingredients thoroughly.
4. Add the lentils to the crock pot as well.
5. Slow cook it for 6 hours.
6. After six hours, if the lentils are undercooked, then turn the setting to high and wait until it gets finely cooked.
7. Now, blend half portion of the lentils.
8. Do not blend the potatoes and add back the blended lentils into the crockpot.
9. Stir them well with the potatoes.
10. Season the stew with raisins, plain yogurt, and cilantro
11. Serve hot.

Henry Wilson

Nutritional values:

Calories: 535 | Carbohydrate: 85.9g | Protein: 37.5g | Fat: 4.1g | Dietary Fiber: 33.8g | Cholesterol: 2mg | Sodium: 1994mg | Potassium: 1915mg | Sugars: 12.8g

10. Crock Pot Mediterranean Chickpeas Stew

(Perfect Mediterranean Diet recipe)

Preparation: 10 minutes | Cooking: 4 hours | Servings: 6

Ingredients:

- Minced garlic - 3 cloves
- Chopped white onion - 1 medium
- Red bell pepper,
- chopped - 1
- Butternut squash, chopped – 1 small
- Drained and rinsed chickpeas - 15 ounces

- Red lentils - ¾ cup
- Tomato sauce - 15 ounces
- Turmeric - 1 teaspoon
- Freshly grated ginger - 1 teaspoon
- Smoked paprika - 1 teaspoon
- Cumin - 1 teaspoon
- Salt - ½ teaspoon
- Pepper - ½ teaspoon
- Cinnamon - ½ teaspoon
- Vegetable broth - 3 cups

For Serving:

- Arugula, chopped - ¼ cup
- Cooked quinoa - ¼ cup
- Coconut yogurt - ½ cup

Cooking directions:

1. Chop butternut squash into bite size and keep aside.
2. Put all the ingredients into the slow cooker.
3. Combine the ingredients thoroughly.
4. Cover the cooker and slow cook for 7 hours.
5. For having a thick stew, open the lid one hour before the set time of cooking and let it cook open.
6. Before serving spread chopped quinoa, arugula over the stew and the yogurt.

Nutritional values:

Calories: 178 | Carbohydrate: 37g | Protein: 8g |Dietary Fiber: 11g | Potassium: 986mg | Sodium: 741mg |Sugars: 8g

VEGETABLES

---

1. Crock Pot Mediterranean Rice & Vegetables

(Perfect Mediterranean Diet recipe)

Preparation: 5 minutes | Cooking: 8 hours | Servings: 6

Henry Wilson

Ingredients:

- Diced onion - 1
- Rice - 2 cups
- Diced tomatoes - 15 ounces
- Diced green bell pepper - 1
- Garlic powder - 1½ teaspoon
- Vegetable broth - 1¾ cups
- Onion water - 1 teaspoon
- Chili powder - 2 teaspoons
- Salsa - ¼ cup

Cooking directions:

1. Put diced onion, rice, diced tomatoes, bell pepper, and vegetable broth into the crockpot.
2. Combine the ingredients thoroughly.
3. Stir in chili powder, garlic powder, salsa, and onion powder.
4. Cover up the crockpot and slow cook for eight hours.
5. Stir again before serving.

Nutritional values:

Calories: 271 | Carbohydrate: 57 | Protein: 7.2g |Fat: 1.2g | Cholesterol: 0mg |Dietary Fiber: 2.9g |Sodium: 305mg |Sugars: 4.5g | Potassium: 420mg

2. Slow Cooker Spanish Chickpeas

(Perfect Mediterranean Diet recipe)

Preparation: 12 minutes | Cooking: 5 hours 10 minutes | Servings: 6

Ingredients:

- Peeled and diced potatoes - 2 medium
- Rinsed and drained chickpeas - 15½ ounces
- Onion, chopped - 1 medium
- Diced tomatoes with juice - 28 ounces
- Garlic, grated - 2 cloves
- Smoked paprika, sweet – 2 teaspoons

- Pepper - ½ teaspoon
- Baby spinach - 4 cups
- Extra virgin olive oil - 4 tablespoons
- Salt - 1 teaspoon

Cooking directions:

1. In slow cooker combine potatoes, chickpeas, onion, tomatoes, paprika, garlic, and salt thoroughly.
2. Close the lid and slow cook for five hours.
3. Add the baby spinach and continue cooking for 10 minutes until the spinach becomes wilted.
4. Before serving, season with pepper and salt as per your taste.
5. Drizzle olive oil before serving.

Nutritional values:

Calories: 330 | Carbohydrate: 49g | Protein: 11g | Fat: 11g | Dietary Fiber: 10g | Cholesterol: 0.0mg | Sodium: 758mg

3. Mediterranean Vegetable Curry

(Perfect Mediterranean Diet recipe)

Preparation: 35 minutes | Cooking: 6 hours | Servings: 6

Ingredients:

- Onion, finely chopped - 1 medium
- Vegetable oil - 1 tablespoon
- Ground coriander - 3 teaspoons
- Minced garlic - 4 cloves
- Ground turmeric - 1 teaspoon
- Ground ginger - 1 teaspoon
- Ground cinnamon - 1½ teaspoon
- Tomato paste - 2 tablespoons
- Cayenne pepper - ½ teaspoon
- Rinsed and drained chickpeas - 15 ounces

- Tomato paste - 2 tablespoons
- Cauliflower florets, fresh - 3 cups
- Peeled sweet potatoes - 3 cups
- Chopped tomatoes - 2 medium
- Cut carrots, sized to ¾" pieces - 4 medium
- Seeded tomatoes, chopped – 2 medium
- Light coconut milk - 1 cup
- Chicken broth - 2 cups
- Salt - ½ teaspoon
- Pepper - ½ teaspoon
- Minced fresh cilantro - ¼ cup
- Lime wedges – 3
- Plain yogurt - ½ cup

Cooking directions:

1. Heat a large skillet and pour oil at medium temperature.
2. Sauté onion for 5 minutes until it turns light brown.
3. Add spices and garlic to the skillet and keep stirring for one minute.
4. Stir in the tomato paste and continue cooking for a minute.
5. Transfer this mixture into a six-quart slow cooker.
6. Mash the beans until it becomes smooth and add it to the slow cooker.
7. Add the vegetables, beans, coconut milk, broth, salt, and pepper.
8. Close the lid and slow cook for six hours.
9. Sprinkle some cilantro over the dish, after cooking.
10. Serve along with lime wedges and top with yogurt.

Nutritional values:

Calories: 304 | Carbohydrate: 49g | Protein: 9g | Fat: 8g | Dietary Fiber: 12g | Sugar: 12g | Cholesterol: 2mg | Sodium: 696mg.

4. Italian Crock Pot Vegetable Dish

(Perfect Mediterranean Diet recipe)

Preparation: 15 minutes | Cooking: 9 hours | Servings: 5

Ingredients:

- Drained and rinsed cannellini beans - 1 can
- Olive oil - 1 teaspoon
- Diced fresh tomatoes - 1½ cup
- Drained and rinsed green beans - 1 can
- Peeled and quartered garlic - 2 cloves
- Quartered yellow onion - 1 medium
- Thickly sliced zucchini - 2 small

- Ground oregano - 1 tablespoon
- Celery - 2 stalks
- Diced and peeled eggplant - 1
- Black pepper - 1 dash

Cooking directions:

1. Grease the bottom of the crockpot with olive oil.
2. Put all the ingredients into the crockpot.
3. Combine the ingredients.
4. Cover the crock pot and slow cook for nine hours.
5. Once it gets thoroughly cooked, season it before serving.
6. Serve hot.

Nutritional values:

Calories: 68 | Carbohydrate: 13.5g | Protein: 2.9g | Fat: 1.5g | Dietary Fiber: 5.8g | Cholesterol: 0.0mg | Sodium: 19mg |Sugars: 6.6g |Potassium: 616mg

5. Mediterranean Vegetable Lasagna

(Perfect Mediterranean Diet recipe)

Preparation: 25 minutes | Cooking: 6 hours | Servings: 9

Ingredients:

- Uncooked whole wheat lasagna noodles - 12
- Marinara sauce - 32 ounces
- Skim ricotta cheese - 24 ounces
- Chopped spinach, frozen and liquid squeezed - 16 ounces
- Mushrooms - 12 ounces
- Mozzarella cheese - 2 pounds
- Cherry tomatoes - 3 ounces
- Chopped fresh parsley - ½ cup

- Salt - 1 teaspoon

Cooking directions:

1. In a medium bowl put spinach, ricotta cheese, salt and combine.
2. Spread half a cup of tomato sauce into the bottom of a 6-quart slow cooker.
3. Break the noodles and layer a portion of it on the tomato sauce.
4. On top of the noodles layer ricotta mixture, along with one-third portions of mushrooms, and one-third portions of mozzarella cheese, and a cup of marinara sauce.
5. Above this layer add another portion of broken noodles.
6. Again layer mozzarella cheese, tomato sauce, and cherry tomatoes.
7. Repeat the layering process until you can make 3 layers.
8. Close the lid and slow cook 6 hours.
9. Once the cooking is over, allow it to settle for 30 minutes.
10. Garnish it with chopped parsley while serving.

Nutritional values:

Calories: 510 | Carbohydrate: 21g | Protein: 34g | Fat: 31g | Dietary Fiber: 4g | Sodium: 1410mg |Potassium: 640mg |Sugars: 11g

6. Crock Pot Tortellini Stew

(Perfect Mediterranean Diet recipe)

Preparation: 15 minutes | Cooking: 8 hours | Servings: 8

Ingredients:

- Zucchini cut into one-inch slices - 2 medium
- Finely chopped onion - 1 small
- Diced tomatoes, undrained - 28 ounces
- Vegetable broth – 29 ounces
- Great Northern Beans - 15½ ounces
- Dried basil leaves - 1 tablespoon
- Pepper - ¼ teaspoon
- Uncooked dry cheese filled tortellini - 8 ounces
- Salt - ¼ teaspoon

Cooking directions:

1. Put onion, vegetable broth, zucchini, great northern beans, tomatoes, pepper and salt into a 6-quart slow cooker. Combine it thoroughly.
2. Close the slow cooker and slow cook for 8 hours.
3. Twenty minutes before serving, stir in tortellini and basil.
4. Now put on high heat for 20 minutes until the tortellini becomes tender.
5. Serve hot.

Nutritional values:

Calories: 170 | Carbohydrate: 26g | Protein: 9g | Fat: 3g | Dietary Fiber: 5g | Sodium: 760mg | Cholesterol: 4mg | Sugars: 4g

7. Slow Cooker Spinach Lasagna

(Perfect Mediterranean Diet recipe)

Preparation: 30 minutes | Cooking: 6 hours | Servings: 8

Ingredients:

- Canned diced tomatoes, undrained - 14½ ounces
- Organic tomato basil paste sauce - 25½ ounces
- Coarsely chopped yellow bell pepper - 1
- Red pepper, crushed - ¼ teaspoon
- Uncooked lasagna noodles - 9
- Thinly sliced zucchini - 1

- Shredded skimmed mozzarella cheese - 6 ounces
- Light ricotta cheese - 1¼ cups
- Coarsely chopped fresh baby spinach - 4 ounces

Cooking directions:

1. Spray some cooking spray in the bottom of a 6-quart slow cooker.
2. In a medium bowl mix tomatoes, pasta sauce, bell pepper, crushed red pepper, and zucchini.
3. Spread a cup of tomato mixture on the bottom part of the slow cooker.
4. Layer the three lasagna noodles over the tomato mixture. Break the noodles so that you can easily layer the noodles.
5. Layer half portion of the ricotta cheese on top of the noodles.
6. Sprinkle half the quantity of spinach and 1/4 cup of mozzarella cheese above the layer.
7. Top it with one-third portion of tomato sauce mixture.
8. Repeat the layering process of noodles, cheese, and spinach for at least three layers.
9. Cover the slow cooker and slow cook for 6 hours until the noodles become tender.
10. Before serving, sprinkle mozzarella all over the lasagna and let it the cheese start melting.

Nutritional values:

Calories: 440 | Carbohydrate: 37g | Protein: 25g | Sugars: 21g | Fat: 22g | Dietary Fiber: 8g | Sodium: 1090mg | Cholesterol: 70mg | Potassium: 1290mg

8. Crock Pot Mediterranean Egg Plant Dish

(Perfect Mediterranean Diet recipe)

Preparation: 15 minutes | Cooking: 9 hours | Servings: 8

Ingredients:

- Diced onion - 1
- Peeled and cubed eggplants - 3 medium
- Diced tomatoes - 1 can
- Diced carrots - 2
- Veg oil - 3 tablespoons
- Tomato paste - 1 tablespoon
- Salt - ¼ teaspoon
- Pepper - ½ teaspoon
- Paprika – as required
- Water – as needed

- Cilantro chopped - ¼ cup

Cooking directions:

1. In a large bowl put cubed eggplants, add water and salt. Stir it so that it can remove the bitter taste of eggplants.
2. Pour oil into a saucepan and bring to medium heat.
3. Put the chopped onion and sauté until it turns light brown and keeps it aside.
4. Now put canned tomatoes, tomato paste, and paprika into a 6-quart slow cooker.
5. Remove the eggplants from the water and wash it under running tap water.
6. Now put the eggplants along with the chopped carrots into the slow cooker.
7. Transfer the sautéed onion into the slow cooker and combine all the ingredients.
8. Add a sufficient quantity of water to cook the vegetables, or until the eggplants and carrots get entirely immersed.
9. Add pepper and salt as per your taste required.
10. Set slow cooker for 9 hours.
11. Garnish with chopped cilantro before serving.
12. Serve hot with rice and salad.

Nutritional values:

Calories: 63 | Carbohydrate: 4.1g | Protein: 0.6g | Sugars: 2.2g | Fat: 5.2g | Dietary Fiber: 1g | Sodium: 88mg | Cholesterol: 0mg |Sugars: 2.2g |Potassium: 144mg

9. Slow Cooker Ratatouille

(Perfect Mediterranean Diet recipe)

Preparation: 25 minutes | Cooking: 6 hours | Servings: 6

Ingredients:

- Eggplant, cut into ¾" size - 1 medium
- Tomato paste - 2 tablespoons
- Olive oil - 3 tablespoons
- Plum tomatoes, medium dice – 1 pound
- Freshly ground black pepper - ¼ teaspoon
- Yellow bell pepper cut into ¼ inch slices - 1 large
- Yellow summer squash, cut into 3/4 inch pieces- 8 ounces
- Garlic, finely sliced - 4 large cloves

- Bay leaf - 1
- Onion sliced into half - 1 large
- Fresh thyme leaves, chopped - 1 tablespoon
- Salt - 1½ teaspoons
- Fresh basil leaves, cut in ribbon size - for garnish

Cooking directions:

1. In a large bowl put eggplant, one teaspoon salt and add water.
2. Stir it and keep aside. Drain after 30 minutes.
3. Rinse it under running tap water and place the eggplant over a paper towel.
4. Take a new bowl and whisk tomato paste, oil and the remaining salt along with black pepper.
5. Combine the drained eggplant, zucchini or squash, tomatoes, onion, bell pepper, thyme, garlic in a slow cooker.
6. Add the tomato-oil paste mixture into the slow cooker and combine.
7. Add bay leaf.
8. Cover and slow cook for 4 hours until the vegetable becomes tender.
9. After four hours, open up the lid and cook for one more hour to let the extra liquid evaporate.
10. Discard the bay leaf before serving.
11. Garnish with fresh basil leaves before serving.

Nutritional Value:

Calories: 130 | Carbohydrate: 15g | Protein: 3g | Sugars: 9g | Fat: 8g | Dietary Fiber: 5g | Sodium: 280mg | Cholesterol: 0mg

10. Slow Cooker Beans Chili

(Perfect Mediterranean Diet recipe)

Preparation: 15 minutes | Cooking: 7 hours | Servings: 6

Ingredients:

- Yellow onion, chopped - 1 large1
- Olive oil, extra virgin - 2 tablespoons
- Red sweet pepper, cored and chopped - 1 medium
- Garlic, minced - 2 large cloves
- Celery stalk, finely chopped - 1 medium
- Yellow sweet pepper, cored and chopped - 1 medium
- Chili powder - 1½ tablespoons
- Cumin - 1 teaspoon
- Baked beans with liquid - 28 ounces

- Carrot peeled and sliced into a ¼ inch - 1 large
- Tomatoes, drained and diced - 28 ounces
- Corn Kernels fresh or frozen - 15 ounces
- Black beans rinsed and drained - 15 ounces
- Kosher salt - ¼ teaspoons
- Unsweetened coconut milk - ¾ cup

For Garnishing:

- Lime zest - ½ teaspoon
- Fresh parsley leaves, chopped - ¼ cup
- Greek yogurt - ½ cup
- Cheddar cheese - ½ cup

Cooking directions:

1. Take a large skillet and heat olive oil on medium heat.
2. Add garlic and onion to the skillet and sauté it until it becomes soft.
3. Add celery, red and yellow sweet pepper, chili powder, cumin and stir for about 3 minutes.
4. Now transfer all these ingredients into a 6-quart slow cooker.
5. Stir to combine all these ingredients.
6. Cover the lid and slow cook for 7 hours.
7. Before serving, garnish using lime zest, fresh Italian parsley leaves, cheddar cheese, and Greek yogurt.

Nutritional values:

Calories: 720 | Carbohydrate: 94g | Protein: 47g | Sugars: 35g | Fat: 22g | Dietary Fiber: 22g | Sodium: 2780mg | Cholesterol: 25mg | Potassium: 1930mg

Soup

1. Slow Cooker Lentil & Ham Soup

Preparation: 20 minutes | Cooking: 11 hours| Servings: 6

Ingredients:

- Chopped celery - 1 cup
- Dried lentils - 1 cup
- Chopped onion - 1 cup

- Chopped carrots - 1 cup
- Cooked ham, chopped - 1½ cups
- Minced garlic - 2 cloves
- Dried thyme - ¼ teaspoon
- Dried basil - ½ teaspoon
- Bay leaf - 1
- Dried oregano - 1/2 teaspoon
- Chicken broth - 32 ounces
- Black pepper - ¼ teaspoon
- Tomato sauce - 8 teaspoons
- Water - 1 cup

Cooking directions:

1. Put celery, lentils, onion, carrots, ham, and garlic in a 4-quart slow cooker and combine thoroughly.
2. Season the ingredients with thyme, basil, bay leaf, oregano, and pepper.
3. Pour chicken broth and stir well.
4. Now add the tomato sauce and water into the slow cooker.
5. Close the lid and slow cook for 11 hours.
6. Remove bay leaf before serving.
7. Serve hot.

Nutritional values:

Calories: 222 | Carbohydrate: 26.3g | Protein: 15.1g | Fat: 6.1g | Sugars: 4g | Dietary Fiber: 11.4g | Cholesterol: 20mg | Sodium: 1170mg | Potassium: 594mg

2. Beef Barley Vegetable Soup

Preparation: 20 minutes | Cooking: 5 hours 30 minutes|
Servings: 10

Ingredients:

- Barley - ½ cup
- Beef chuck roast - 3 pounds
- Oil - 2 tablespoons
- Bay leaf - 1
- Chopped celery - 3 stalks
- Chopped carrots - 3
- Mixed vegetables - 16 ounces
- Chopped onion - 1
- Beef bouillon - 4 cubes
- Water - 4 cups

- Ground black pepper - ¼ teaspoon
- White sugar - 1 tablespoon
- Salt - ¼ teaspoon
- Stewed tomatoes, diced - 28 ounces

Cooking directions:

1. Take a slow cooker and
2. Cook chuck roast in the slow cooker at high heat for 5 until it becomes soft.
3. Add a bay leaf and barley into the slow cooker one hour before the end of cooking.
4. Remove the meat and chop it into small pieces.
5. Discard the bay leaf as well.
6. Set the broth, beef and the barley aside.
7. Pour oil in a large cooking pot and bring it on medium heat.
8. Sauté celery, onion, frozen mixed vegetables, and carrots until they become soft.
9. Add beef bouillon cubes, water, pepper, sugar, beef or barley mixture, tomatoes.
10. Boil the mix and reduce the heat and let it simmer for about ten to twenty minutes.
11. Season it with salt and pepper before serving.

Nutritional values:

Calories: 321 | Carbohydrate: 22.4g | Protein: 20g | Fat: 17.3g | Sugars: 6g | Dietary Fiber: 5.1g | Cholesterol: 62mg | Sodium: 605mg | Potassium: 552mg

3. Slow Cooker Corn Chowder

Preparation: 15 minutes | Cooking: 4 hours | Servings: 8

Ingredients:

- Cream style corn - 14¾ ounces
- Milk - 3 cups
- Chopped green chilies - 4 ounces
- Condensed mushroom cream soup - 10¾ ounces
- Hash brown potatoes, frozen & shredded - 2 cups
- Frozen corn - 2 cups
- Chopped onion - 1 large
- Cooked ham, cubed - 2 cups

- Hot sauce - 2 tablespoons
- Butter - 2 tablespoons
- Chili powder - 1 teaspoon
- Dried parsley - 2 teaspoons
- Salt - ¼ teaspoon
- Ground black pepper - ½ teaspoon

Cooking directions:

1. Stir in cream-style corn, milk, chopped green chilies, cream of mushroom soup, hash brown potatoes, frozen corn, ham, butter, onion, parsley, chili powder and hot sauce in a slow cooker.
2. Season the soup with black pepper and salt as per your taste.
3. Cover the cooker and slow cook for 6 hours.
4. Serve hot.

Nutritional values:

Calories: 376 | Carbohydrate: 47.1g | Protein: 14.9g | Fat: 18.7g | Sugars: 12g | Dietary Fiber: 3.6g | Cholesterol: 34mg | Sodium: 1716mg | Potassium: 787mg

4. Slow Cooker Chicken Posole

(Perfect Mediterranean Diet recipe)

Preparation: 10 minutes | Cooking: 6 hours 40 minutes | Servings: 6

Ingredients:

- Skinless, boneless chicken breasts - 3
- Chicken broth, low sodium - 4 cups
- Chopped white onion - 1
- Chopped poblano peppers - 2
- Cumin - 1 tablespoon

- Minced garlic - 2 cloves
- Chili powder - 2 teaspoons
- Oregano - 1 tablespoon
- Kosher salt - 2 teaspoons
- Ground black pepper, fresh - ½ teaspoon
- Drained hominy - 15 ounces

For Garnish:

- Sliced green cabbage - ¾ cup
- Thinly sliced radish - ½ cup
- Fresh cilantro, chopped - ¼ cup

Cooking directions:

1. In a slow cooker combine all items, except the ingredients for garnish and hominy.
2. Cover and slow cook for 8 hours.
3. After cooking, take the chicken out of the slow cooker and shred it using a fork
4. Return it to the slow cooker along with hominy.
5. Cook it further 30 minutes.
6. Garnish it with cabbage, radish, and cilantro before serving.

Nutritional values:

Calories: 105 | Carbohydrate: 16.6g | Protein: 5.5g | Fat: 2.1g | Sugars: 3.9g | Dietary Fiber: 3.6g | Cholesterol: 0mg | Sodium: 1451mg | Potassium: 317mg

5. Crock Pot Butternut Squash Soup

(Perfect Mediterranean Diet recipe)

Preparation: 40 minutes | Cooking: 8 hours | Servings: 6

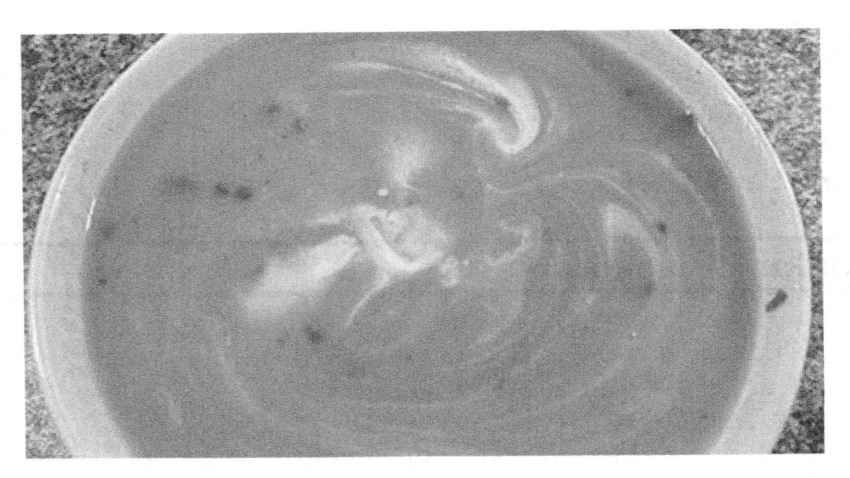

Ingredients:

- Chicken broth, low sodium - 4 cups
- Diced butternut squash - 6 cups
- Halved and quartered onion - 1 medium
- Peeled and diced carrots - 2 medium
- Cinnamon - 1 teaspoon
- Chipotle peppers in adobe sauce - 2
- Pepper - ½ teaspoon
- Salt - 1 teaspoon
- Yogurt - ¼ cup

Cooking directions:

1. Put all the ingredients in the slow cooker and combine.
2. Close the lid and slow cook for 8 hours.
3. After cooking, make a puree by using an immersion blender.
4. Check salt and other seasonings as per your taste.
5. If you want to reduce the consistency add more chicken broth.
6. Drizzle with plain yogurt before serving.

Nutritional values:

Calories: 142 | Carbohydrate: 33.1g | Protein: 4.8g | Fat: 0.6g | Sugars: 8.7g | Dietary Fiber: 6.6g | Sodium: 1246mg

6. Slow Cooker Mediterranean Chicken Soup

(Perfect Mediterranean Diet recipe)

Preparation: 10 minutes | Cooking: 3 hours| Servings: 11

Ingredients:

- Boneless chicken breast – 1pound
- Chicken broth - 3 cups
- Lite coconut milk - 14 ounces
- Red curry paste - 4 ounces
- Peanut butter - ½ cup
- Soy sauce, low sodium - 5 tablespoons
- Fish sauce - 2 tablespoons
- Garlic, minced - 4 cloves

- Dark brown sugar - 2 tablespoons
- Red pepper flakes - ½ teaspoon
- Ground ginger - 1 teaspoon
- Diced yellow onion - 1
- Red bell pepper, chopped - 1
- Carrots, diagonally sliced - 1 cup
- Broccoli, sliced florets - 1 head
- Sliced mushrooms - 8 ounces
- Lime juice - 3 tablespoons
- Salt - ¼ teaspoon

For Garnish:

- Chopped peanuts - ¼ cup
- Chopped cilantro - ¼ cup

Cooking directions:

1. Slightly oil the bottom of the crockpot and stir in broth, coconut milk, curry paste, peanut butter, soy sauce, fish sauce, garlic, brown sugar, red pepper flakes, salt, and ginger
2. Put onion, chicken breasts, pepper, carrots, broccoli, mushrooms and mix thoroughly.
3. Cover the lid and slow cook for 8 hours.
4. Remove the cooked chicken into a bowl and chop into small pieces.
5. Put it back into the soup.
6. Add lime juice and stir.
7. Season with curry paste, salt and red pepper flakes as per your taste, if required.
8. Garnish with chopped peanuts and cilantro before serving.

Henry Wilson

Nutritional values:

Calories: 239 | Carbohydrate: 16g | Protein: 15g | Fat: 12g | Sugars: 7g | Dietary Fiber: 3g | Cholesterol: 26mg | Sodium: 877mg |Potassium: 623mg

7. Slow Cooker Chicken & Vegetable Soup

(Perfect Mediterranean Diet recipe)

Preparation: 15 minutes | Cooking: 8 hours| Servings: 8

Ingredients:

- Chicken broth, low sodium - 4 cups
- Fat trimmed and skinned chicken breasts - 1½ pounds
- Parsnips, ¼" sliced - 3 medium
- Carrots, ¼" sliced - 3 medium
- Chopped onion - 1 medium
- Peeled & finely sliced celery - 2 stalks
- Yellow curry powder - 1 teaspoon
- Parmesan rind 2" piece - ½ cup
- Frozen peas - 1 cup

- Kosher salt - ¼ teaspoon
- Ground black pepper - ½ teaspoon
- Fresh dill fronds, chopped - ½ cup loosely packed

For Garnish:

- Lemon, grated – 1 tablespoon
- Grated Parmesan - ¼ cup

Cooking directions:

1. Put all the ingredients, except the garnish into 6-quart slow cooker.
2. Close the lid and slow cook for 8 hours.
3. After cooking, take out the chicken breast and allow it to cool for some time.
4. Shred the meat after cooling and discard the bone.
5. Now put back the shredded chicken meat into the slow cooker.
6. Add dill.
7. Season the soup with pepper and salt as per your taste.
8. While serving garnish it with lemon juice and grated parmesan.

Nutritional values:

Calories: 212 | Carbohydrate: 8.5g | Protein: 27.6g | Fat: 7.2g | Sugars: 2.7g | Dietary Fiber: 2.6g | Cholesterol: 77mg | Sodium: 231mg |Potassium: 441mg

8. Crock Pot Mediterranean Beef Soup

Preparation: 20 minutes | Cooking: 9 | Servings: 8

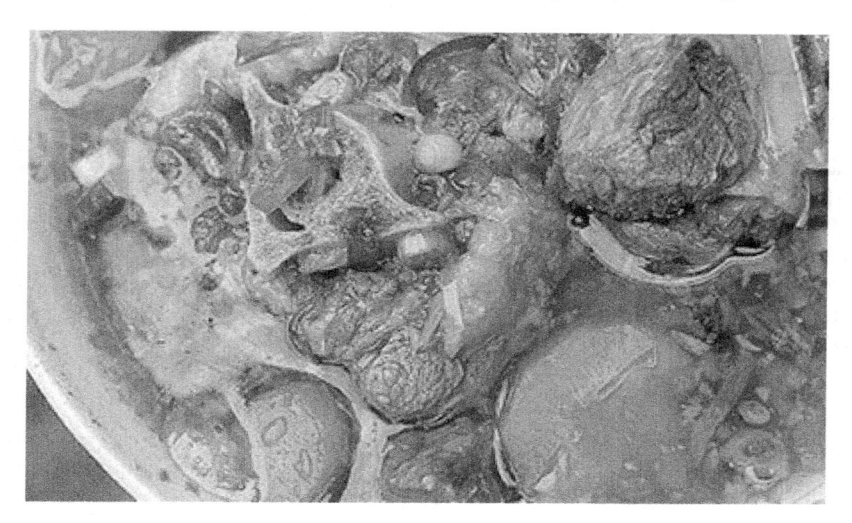

Ingredients:

- Stew beef, cut to 1" size – 2 pound
- Carrots, chopped – 1 cup
- Onion, diced – 1
- Beef broth – 30 ounces
- Oregano – 1 teaspoon
- Italian diced tomatoes – 29 ounces
- Onion powder – 2 teaspoon
- Drained beans – 30 ounces
- Salt - ½ teaspoon
- Ground black pepper - ½ teaspoon
- Parmesan cheese, shredded - ¼ cup

Cooking directions:

1. Drain the beans.
2. Cut the onions and carrots.
3. Put all the ingredients in a slow cooker, except parmesan cheese.
4. Slow cook for 9 hours.
5. Before serving, garnish it with parmesan.

Nutritional values:

Calories: 230 | Carbohydrate: 11.3g | Protein: 29.4g | Fat: 7.6g | Dietary Fiber: 4.4g |Sodium: 369mg |Cholesterol: 0mg |Potassium: 388mg |Sugars: 3.3g

9. Slow Cooker Split Pea

Preparation: 5 minutes | Cooking: 6 hours | Servings: 6

Ingredients:

- Hambone - 1½ pounds
- Dried split peas - 16 ounces
- Diced yellow onion - 1
- Diced carrots – 3
- Diced shallot - 1
- Minced garlic - 3 cloves
- Diced celery - 2 stalks
- Dried thyme - 1 teaspoon
- Minced garlic - 3 cloves
- Bay leaf - 1
- Ground black pepper - ½ teaspoon

- Chicken broth, low sodium - 6 cups

Cooking directions:

1. Combine carrots, split peas, shallot, yellow onion, garlic, celery, pepper, thyme, chicken stock and bay leaf in a slow cooker
2. Add ham bone and stir.
3. Cover the lid and slow cook for 6 hours.
4. Remove the ham from the slow cooker and shred into small pieces using a fork
5. Discard the bone.
6. Put back ham meat back into the slow cooker.
7. Discard the bay leaf and serve hot.

Nutritional values:

Calories: 321 | Carbohydrate: 54g | Protein: 23g | Fat: 2g | Sugars: 8g | Dietary Fiber: 20g | Potassium: 1088mg | Sodium: 104mg

10. Slow Cooker Fish Soup

(Perfect Mediterranean Diet recipe)

Preparation: 20 minutes | Cooking: 6 hours 20 minutes|
Servings: 6

Ingredients:

- Shrimp, deveined medium – 1 pound
- Cubed cod fillets - 1 pound
- Chopped green bell pepper - ½
- Chopped onion - 1
- Drained and diced tomatoes - 14½ ounces

- Minced garlic - 2 cloves
- Tomato sauce - 8 ounces
- Chicken broth - 14 ounces
- Sliced black olives - ¼ cup
- Canned mushrooms - 2½ ounces
- Dry white wine - ½ cup
- Orange juice - ½ cup
- Dried basil - 1 teaspoon
- Bay leaves - 2
- Ground black pepper - ⅛ teaspoon
- Crushed fennel seed - ¼ teaspoon

Cooking directions:

1. In a slow cooker combine garlic, green bell pepper, chicken broth, tomatoes, mushrooms, tomato sauce, orange juice, olives, bay leaves, wine, fennel seeds, dried basil, and pepper.
2. Close the lid and slow cook 4½ hours.
3. Put cod and shrimp.
4. Stir thoroughly.
5. Cook it for about 30 minutes or until the shrimp become opaque.
6. Discard the bay leaf before serving.

Nutritional values:

Calories: 222 | Carbohydrate: 11.9g | Protein: 31.3g | Fat: 3g | Sugars: 7g | Dietary Fiber: 2.2g | Cholesterol: 151mg | Sodium: 1231mg | Potassium: 706mg

Pizza & Pasta

1. Crock Pot Pizza and Pasta

Preparation: 10 minutes | Cooking: 3¾ hours | Servings: 4

Ingredients:

- Chicken broth, low sodium, divided into - 3½ cups and 1 tablespoon

- Lean ground beef - ½ pound
- Turkey pepperonis - ½ cup
- Organic pizza sauce - 1½ cups
- Chopped and cooked ham - ½ cup
- Salt - ¾ teaspoon
- Italian seasoning - 2 teaspoons
- Gluten-free rotini pasta - 8 ounces
- Pepper - as per taste required
- Mozzarella cheese - 1 cup
- Non - GMO Cornstarch - ½ tablespoon

Cooking directions:

1. Crush the lean ground beef into the slow cooker.
2. Add a cup of broth to the slow cooker, reserve the rest for later use.
3. Cook the beef on slow cook mode for three hours.
4. After cooking, add about ¾ cups of pizza sauce, ham, pepperonis, salt, Italian seasoning and pepper into the slow cooker.
5. Mix them well together.
6. Next, add the pasta and the remaining two and a half cups of broth to the slow cooker.
7. Take a small bowl and whisk the remaining chicken broth along with the cornstarch until it becomes smooth.
8. Pour this mixture into the slow cooker.
9. Cover the slow cooker and let it cook under high heat for an hour or until the pasta gets thoroughly cooked
10. Do not overcook the noodles, and it is highly recommended to check with the consistency level of the noodles by opening the slow cooker when the timer hits forty-five minutes.
11. Once the noodles are cooked well, pour the remaining ¾ cups of pizza sauce along with cheese.
12. Serve hot.

Nutritional values:

Calories: 282 | Carbohydrate: 34.8g | Protein: 20.2g | Sugars: 4.3g | Fat: 8.2g | Dietary Fiber: 5g | Cholesterol: 44.6mg | Sodium: 1130mg | Potassium: 300.3mg

2. Slow Cooker Beef Pizza

Preparation: 2 minutes | Cooking: 4 hours | Servings: 6

Ingredients:

- Rigatoni pasta - 8 ounces
- Ground beef - 1½ pounds
- Shredded mozzarella cheese - 16 ounces
- Pizza sauce - 14 ounces
- Tomato soup, condensed cream in a can - 10¾ ounces
- Sliced pepperoni sausage - 8 ounces

Cooking directions:

1. Boil salt water in a large pot.
2. Cook pasta in it for about 10 minutes
3. Add pasta to it and let it cook for about eight to ten minutes so that it will remain firm and smooth to bite
4. Drain the pasta and set it aside.
5. Now cook beef in a large skillet on medium high heat, until it becomes brown on all sides.
6. Layer the beef in the slow cooker and on top layer mozzarella cheese, cooked pasta, and condensed cream of tomato sauce, soup and pepperoni.
7. Slow cook the ingredients for 4 hours.
8. Serve hot.

Nutritional values:

Calories: 820 | Carbohydrate: 50.9g | Protein: 53.8g | Sugars: 12g |Fat: 43.3g | Dietary Fiber: 3.7g | Cholesterol: 154mg | Sodium: 2181mg | Potassium: 413mg

3. Slow Cooker Deep Dish Pizza

Preparation: 10 minutes | Cooking: 2 hours | Servings: 4

Ingredients:

- Pizza sauce - ⅓ cup
- Refrigerated Pizza crust - 11 ounces
- Cooked and crumbled sausage - ¼ pound
- Shredded mozzarella cheese – 1 cup
- Sliced pepperoni - ½ cup
- Non-stick cooking spray – as required

Cooking directions:

1. Drizzle non-stick cooking spray in a 4-quart slow cooker.

2. Spread out pizza dough and fold in half crosswise and place in the slow cooker.
3. Press the pizza to the bottom by keeping the edges one inch up.
4. Now evenly spread the pizza sauce on the dough.
5. Layer it with half portions of sausage, cheese, and pepperoni
6. Repeat the process by adding the remaining pepperoni, sausage, and cheese.
7. Close the cooker lit and slow cook for 2 hours until the crust edges turn golden brown, and the cheese melted.
8. Remove the pizza from the slow cooker and transfer it to a cutting board
9. Cut the pizza into four slices and serve hot.

Nutritional values:

Calories: 430 | Carbohydrate: 39g | Protein: 19g | Sugars: 4g |Fat: 22g | Dietary Fiber: 1g | Cholesterol: 40mg | Sodium: 920mg | Potassium: 180mg

4. Mediterranean-Italian Style Pork Pizza

Preparation: 15 minutes | Cooking: 5 hours | Servings: 4

Ingredients:

- Thawed, frozen pizza dough – 1 pound
- Italian pork sausage, cooked ½ - pound
- Flour – 1 tablespoon
- Marinara sauce - 1½ cup
- Garlic, minced – 1 clove
- Pepperoni, sliced – 12 slices
- Italian blend cheese, grated - 1½ cup
- Parmesan cheese, grated - ¼ cup
- Parsley, chopped - ¼ cup

Cooking directions:

1. Place a large parchment paper in the crock pot and spread flour.
2. Roll the thawed frozen pizza dough on the flour in an oval shape.
3. The doughs edges should overlap the size of your crockpot and keep it aside.
4. Now heat a skillet on medium high temperature and cook the pork sausage.
5. While cooking, break the sausages into tiny pieces.
6. Stir in minced garlic and continue cooking.
7. Once cooking over keep it aside.
8. Spread the sauce over the pizza crust.
9. Layer over it with cheese.
10. Stretch out the side of the pizza dough, so that the cheese will not sweep out.
11. Now sprinkle the cooked sausage over it.
12. Over the layer, spread the pepperoni.
13. Stretch out the side of the pizza dough, so that the layering will stay within the pizza crust.
14. Now place a large paper towel over the mouth of the crock pot and close the lit firmly.
15. Slow cook for 5 hours.
16. Serve hot by topping with grated parmesan cheese and sprinkling chopped parsley.

Nutritional values:

Calories: 635 | Carbohydrate: 62g | Protein: 30g | Fat: 31g | Dietary Fiber: 3g | Cholesterol: 53mg | Sodium: 1812mg |Sugars: 10g |Potassium: 455mg

5. Slow Cooker Mediterranean Pasta

(Perfect Mediterranean Diet recipe)

Preparation: 10 minutes | Cooking: 4 hours | Servings: 8

Ingredients:

- Pasta – 1 pound
- Minced garlic - 2 cloves
- Chopped onion - 1
- Salt - as per taste required
- Pepper - as per taste required
- Chicken tenders - 1¼ pounds
- Marinara sauce - 25 ounces

- Italian seasoning - 1 teaspoon
- Cream cheese - 12 ounces
- Bay leaves – 2
- Pepper - ¼ teaspoon
- Salt - ¼ teaspoon

Cooking directions:

1. Put garlic, onion, salt, chicken pepper, cream cheese, marinara, bay leaves, and Italian seasoning in a crockpot.
2. Cover and slow cook for 4 hours, until the chicken becomes soft.
3. Shred the chicken with a spoon.
4. Add cream cheese into the sauce and let it melt.
5. Top it with cooked hot pasta.
6. Serve hot.

Nutritional values:

Calories: 465 | Carbohydrate: 50g | Protein: 26g | Sugars: 7g |Fat: 17g | Dietary Fiber: 3g | Cholesterol: 92mg | Sodium: 687mg | Potassium: 760mg

6. Slow Cooker Chicken Parmesan Pasta

(Perfect Mediterranean Diet recipe)

Preparation: 15 minutes | Cooking: 4 hours 30 minutes|
Servings: 8

Ingredients:

- Skinless, boneless chicken breasts - 4
- Dried oregano - 1 teaspoon
- Diced onion - 1
- Dried basil - 1 tablespoon
- Crushed tomatoes - 56 ounces (2 cans)
- Crushed red pepper flakes - ½ teaspoon
- Shredded mozzarella cheese - 1½ cups
- Penne - 1 pound
- Chopped fresh parsley leaves - 2 tablespoons
- Parmesan cheese, shredded - ¼ cup

- Ground black pepper, fresh - ¼ teaspoon
- Kosher salt - ¼ teaspoon
- Dried parsley - 1 teaspoon

Cooking directions:

1. Season the chicken breasts with pepper and salt.
2. Place the chicken breasts into a 6-quart slow cooker.
3. In a large bowl combine onion, crushed tomatoes, basil, parsley, oregano, and red pepper flakes.
4. Stir in this mixture into the slow cooker and gently toss it to combine.
5. Cover the cooker and slow cook for 4 hours.
6. After four hours, remove the chicken breasts from the cooker and shred with a fork.
7. Boil pasta in salted water and drain it.
8. Put back the shredded chicken and add the cooked pasta into the slow cooker and top it up with cheese.
9. Cover the slow cooker and slow cook for 30 minutes until the cheese melts thoroughly.
10. Garnish with freshly chopped parsley before serving.

Nutritional values:

Calories: 455.5 | Carbohydrate: 59.7g | Protein: 36g | Sugars: 2.6g |Fat: 8.5g | Dietary Fiber: 6.2g | Cholesterol: 69mg | Sodium: 503.3mg

7. Slow Cooker Pasta Meat Sauce with Ground Turkey

(Perfect Mediterranean Diet recipe)

Preparation: 15 minutes | Cooking: 8 hours | Servings: 8

Ingredients:

- Turkey, grounded - 1 pound
- Diced onion - 1 medium
- Minced garlic - 6 cloves
- Diced tomatoes - 29 ounces (2 cans)
- Olive oil - 2 tablespoons
- Tomato paste - 2 tablespoons
- Tomato sauce - 14½ ounces (1 can)

- Italian herb seasoning - 2 tablespoons
- Dry red wine - 1/2 cup
- Black pepper, grounded - ¼ teaspoon
- Salt - ½ teaspoon
- Red pepper, crushed - ¼ teaspoon
- Non-stick cooking spray – as required

For Garnish:

- Fresh Italian parsley, chopped - ¼ cup
- Parmesan cheese - ¼ cup

Cooking directions:

1. Spray some non-stick cooking oil in the bottom of the slow cooker.
2. Put onion, olive oil and garlic in a slow bowl and microwave for two minutes at full power.
3. Make sure to stop the microwave at one minute and stir the mixture and then cook it for the remaining one minute.
4. In the slow cooker, put tomato sauce or crushed tomatoes, diced tomatoes, dry red wine, tomato paste, Italian herb seasoning, ground black pepper, salt, and crushed red pepper and combine.
5. Break the ground turkey into chunks and put into the sauce.
6. Tap the turkey chunks with a large spoon so that they should get partially covered with the sauce.
7. Do not stir the turkey.
8. Close the cooker and slow cook for 8 hours.
9. Once the turkey gets finely cooked, stir in the microwave cooked sauce.
10. Sprinkle grated parmesan cheese and chopped parsley before serving.

Nutritional values:

Calories: 201 | Carbohydrate: 11.4g | Protein: 18.9g | Sugars: 6.8g |Fat: 8g | Dietary Fiber: 3.4g

8. Crock Pot Pizza Casserole

Preparation: 15 minutes | Cooking: 5 hours | Servings: 6

Ingredients:

- Low-fat beef, minced - 1 pound
- Onion – 1 small
- Crushed tomatoes - 28 ounces
- Crushed garlic - 2 cloves
- Sliced pepperoni - 4 ounces
- Oregano - 2 teaspoons
- Green pepper - ½ teaspoon
- Pepper - 1 teaspoon
- Divided mozzarella cheese - 2 cups

- Chopped green pepper - ½ teaspoon
- Uncooked pasta - 2 cups
- Water - 1 cup
- Salt - 2 teaspoons

Cooking directions:

1. Chop half of green pepper, onion and keep aside.
2. In a large skillet, over medium heat brown the ground beef.
3. When the beef becomes brown add chopped onions and let it cook for 8 minutes. Stir continuously.
4. When the onion becomes tender, add crushed garlic and stir it for a minute.
5. In a crockpot, add water, crushed tomatoes, oregano, four ounces of sliced pepperoni, salt, pepper, salt, mozzarella cheese, and green pepper
6. Add the uncooked pasta into the slow cooker and mix thoroughly.
7. Now, transfer the cooked ground beef mixture into the slow cooker.
8. Top it up with mozzarella and twelve slices of pepperoni.
9. Close the lid and slow cook for 5 hours or until the edges turn brown in terms of color
10. Serve hot.

Nutritional values:

Calories: 485 | Carbohydrate: 27g | Protein: 33g | Sugars: 6g |Fat: 28g | Dietary Fiber: 4g | Cholesterol: 92mg | Sodium: 1873mg | Potassium: 307mg

9. Slow Cooker Mediterranean Pasta

Preparation: 15 minutes | Cooking: 9 hours 15 minutes | Servings: 4

Ingredients:

- Beef meat, stew type - 1 pound
- Penne pasta - 1½ cups
- Chopped onion - 1/2 cup
- Drained and sliced mushrooms - 4½ ounces
- Drained and chopped artichoke hearts - 14 ounces
- Drained capers - 1 tablespoon
- Balsamic vinegar - 1 tablespoon
- Italian seasoning - 1 teaspoon
- Garlic, dried minced - 1 tablespoon
- Sugar - 1 teaspoon

- Salt - 1 teaspoon
- Olive oil - 1 tablespoon
- Parmesan cheese, grated - ½ cup
- Fresh ground pepper - ¼ teaspoon
- Olive oil – as required

Cooking directions:

1. Sprinkle cooking spray into a four-quart slow cooker.
2. Add beef stew meat, mushrooms, onion, artichoke hearts, tomatoes, drained capers, balsamic vinegar, minced garlic, salt, and Italian seasoning into the slow cooker.
3. Cover the lid and slow cook for 9 hours.
4. Cook the pasta 15 minutes before serving.
5. Put the cooked pasta, oil and pepper in the beef mixture and stir.
6. Serve hot topping with cheese.

Nutritional values:

Calories: 560 | Carbohydrate: 58g | Protein: 35g | Sugars: 8g |Fat: 21g | Dietary Fiber: 13g | Cholesterol: 70mg | Sodium: 1470mg | Potassium: 890mg

10. Robust Mediterranean Sausage & Pasta

Preparation: 15 minutes | Cooking: 6½ hours | Servings: 4

Ingredients:

- Sausage, Italian links, cut into half – 4 ounces each
- Undrained tomatoes and chilies chopped – 10 ounces
- Italian sausage spaghetti sauce – 25.6 ounces
- Onion, chopped – 1 medium
- Green pepper, julienned – 1 large
- Italian seasoning – 1 teaspoon
- Spiral pasta, uncooked – 2 cups
- Garlic, minced – 2 cloves

Henry Wilson

Cooking directions:

1. Brown the sausages in a large non-stick skillet.
2. Transfer the brown sausages into a 4-quarter slow cooker.
3. Now put tomatoes, onion, green pepper, garlic, spaghetti sauce, Italian seasoning and combine.
4. Close the lid and slow cook for 6 hours.
5. Add pasta.
6. Cover and cook again high for 30 minutes to tender the pasta.
7. Serve hot.

Nutritional values:

Calories: 529 | Carbohydrate: 60g | Protein: 23g | Sugars: 19g |Fat: 22g |Cholesterol: 53g | Sodium: 1573mg

Beans & Grain

1. Three Bean Mediterranean Slow Cooker Chili

(Perfect Mediterranean Diet recipe)

Preparation: 10 minutes | Cooking: 12 hours | Servings: 10

Ingredients:

- Ground Turkey breast 99% lean – 1.3 pounds
- Diced tomatoes, drained – 28 ounces
- Onion, small, chopped – 1
- Tomato sauce – 16 ounces
- Chopped chilies in the can – 4½ ounces
- Black beans drained – 15½ ounces
- Chickpeas drained – 15 ounces
- Small red beans, drained – 15½ ounces
- Chili powder – 2 tablespoons
- Cumin – 1 teaspoon

For the topping:

- Chopped fresh cilantro for topping – ½ cup
- Red onion, chopped – ½ cup
- Shredded cheddar - ¼ cup
- Sour cream - ¼ cup
- Avocado pieces - ¼ cup

Cooking directions:

1. Put turkey and onion into a medium-size skillet on medium-high heat. Continue cooking until the turkey becomes brown on all sides.
2. Now, take a slow cooker and transfer the turkey and onion into it.
3. Add beans, tomatoes, chickpeas, chilies, tomato sauce, cumin, and chili powder into the cooker and combine.
4. Slow cook it for 12 hours.
5. Top it with onions, cilantro, avocado pieces, shredded cheddar, and sour cream while serving.

6. Serve it hot.

Nutritional value:

Calories: 231 | Carbohydrates: 27.5g | Protein: 19.5g | Sugar: 6.5g | Total Fat: 5g, Saturated fat: 1.5g | Cholesterol: 42mg | Sodium: 526mg | Fiber: 8g

2. Beans and Barley Stew

(Perfect Mediterranean Diet recipe)

Preparation: 10 minutes | Cooking: 8 hours 10 minutes | Servings: 10

Ingredients:

- Dried bean mix, rinsed (kidney, navy, pinto) – 1 pound
- Dried barley – 8 ounces
- Low sodium chicken broth – 8 cups
- Yellow onion, chopped - 1
- Celery stalks, diced - 3
- Barley – ½ pound
- Carrots, diced - 2

- Garlic, minced – 2 cloves
- Bay leaf – 1
- Fresh thyme – few springs
- Baby spinach – 8 ounces
- Kosher salt – 2 teaspoon
- Water – 2 cups

Cooking directions:

1. In the slow cooker combine bean mix, pepper, carrots, celery, garlic, thyme, onions, bay leaf, and salt.
2. Pour the broth and also 2 cups of water and stir thoroughly.
3. Cover the cooker and slow cook for 7 hours.
4. Now add barely.
5. If the stew consistency is too thick, add some more water.
6. Cover again and cook for 1 more hour.
7. Before serving add spinach and stir.
8. Serve hot.

Nutritional value:

Calories: 262 |Fat: 1.1g | Cholesterol: 0mg | Sodium: 560g | Carbohydrate: 48.8g | Dietary Fiber: 12g | Sugars: 2.4g | Protein: 15.6g |Potassium: 917mg

Henry Wilson

3. Mediterranean Lentils and Rice

(Perfect Mediterranean Diet recipe)

Preparation: 15 minutes | cooking: 8 hours | Servings: 6

Ingredients:

- Brown lentils – 1 cup
- Onion, chopped – 1
- Rice – ½ cup
- Salt – ¾ teaspoon
- Cinnamon – ½ teaspoon
- Ground cumin – 1 tablespoon
- Olive oil – 4½ teaspoons
- Water or homemade vegetable stock or chicken stock – 6 cups

Cooking directions:

1. Pour olive oil in the crock pot.
2. Set the crock pot on high heat.
3. Put onion into it and sauté.
4. After 10-15 minutes, put all the remaining ingredients including water into the crockpot.
5. Cover the crock pot and slow cook for 8 hours.
6. You may stir the dish in between to check whether food is dry or moisturized. Add water if required.
7. Serve hot.

Nutritional value:

Calories: 98| Fat: 3.8g| Cholesterol: 0mg | Sodium: 23mg | Carbohydrate: 14.7 | Dietary Fiber: 0.8g | Sugars: 08g | Protein: 1.5g | Potassium: 63mg

4. Italian-Mediterranean Multi-Bean Soup

(Perfect Mediterranean Diet recipe)

Preparation: 10 minutes | Cooking: 10 hours | Servings: 12

Ingredients:

- Chicken broth – 8¾ cups
- Organic tomato, diced - 14½ ounces
- Dried bean soup – 16 ounces
- Carrots, chopped – 4 medium
- Onion, chopped – 1 large
- Stalks celery, chopped – 3 medium
- Tomato paste – 2 tablespoons
- Pepper – ½ teaspoon

- Italian seasoning – 1 teaspoon
- Salt – 1 teaspoon

Cooking directions:

1. In a 6-quart slow cooker, combine all the ingredients, except tomatoes.
2. Cover the slow cooker, and set low cooking for 10 hours.
3. Add tomatoes and mix them well.
4. Switch from low heat to high heat.
5. Cover the cooker and cook further 15 more minutes or until it becomes hot.
6. Serve hot.

Nutritional value:

Calories: 180 | Carbohydrate: 30g | Dietary Fiber: 5g | Sugars: 3g | Protein: 13g | Fat: 1g | Cholesterol: 0mg | Sodium: 1040 mg | Potassium: 370 mg

5. Mediterranean Slow Cooked Green Beans

(Perfect Mediterranean Diet recipe)

Preparation: 10 minutes | Cooking: 3 hours | Servings: 12

Ingredients:

- Frozen French-style green beans, thawed – 16 cups
- Brown sugar – ½ cup
- Low sodium soy sauce – ¾ teaspoon
- Butter, melted – ½ cup
- Garlic salt – 1½ teaspoons

Cooking directions:

1. Put beans into a 6-quart slow cooker.
2. Stir in other ingredients including sugar, soy sauce, butter, and garlic salt.
7. Cover the cooker and cook the beans for about 3 hours on low heat.
8. Serve hot.

Nutritional values:

Calories: 143 | Carbohydrate: 17g | Sugars: 12g | Fiber: 3g | Protein: 1g | Fat: 8g | Cholesterol: 20 mg | Sodium: 320 mg

6. Slow Cooked Green Beans

Preparation: 15 minutes | Cooking: 3½ hours | Servings: 6

Ingredients:

- Bacon sliced crosswise into ½ inch pieces – 6 slices
- Garlic, minced – 3 cloves
- Onion, sliced lengthwise – 1
- Fresh green beans, trimmed – 2 pounds
- Chicken broth – 3 cups
- Tomato sauce – ¼ cup
- Cayenne pepper – 1 pinch
- Salt - ¼ teaspoon
- Black pepper ground – ¼ teaspoon

Cooking directions:

1. Heat a saucepan on medium heat.
2. Add sliced bacon into the hot pan. Stir and cook it for about 6 minutes until it becomes brown and crispy.
3. Now, add onion into the pan and cook it for about 5 minutes until the onion becomes mushy and golden brown. Let the brown chunks of food at the bottom gets dissolved with the onion's juices.
4. Add tomato sauce and minced garlic into the pan and mix it well. Cook for about 1 more minute until the garlic becomes soft.
5. Take a skillet and add green beans into it and add chicken broth into it.
6. Heat the skillet on high heat and add black pepper, cayenne pepper, and salt into the skillet. Cook the beans until it becomes soft.
7. Now, switch the cooker from high heat to slow cooking mode for 3 hours. Keep stirring the mixture intermittently. If the mixture appears to be dry, pour more water or broth into it.
8. Check the salt and pepper. If required adjust its taste as needed.
9. After adding salt and pepper, cook it further for about 30 minutes.
10. Serve it hot along with its juice.

Nutritional value:

Calories: 124 | Carbohydrate: 16g | Protein: 7.3g | Fat: 4.3g | Cholesterol: 13mg | Sodium: 782 mg | Potassium: 464mg |Sugars: 5g

7. Slow Cooker Moroccan Chickpea Stew

(Perfect Mediterranean Diet recipe)

Preparation: 10 minutes | Cooking: 7 hours | Servings: 6

Ingredients:

- Medium white onion chopped – 1
- Garlic cloves minced – 3
- Red bell pepper chopped – 1
- Small butternut squash peeled and cut into bite-sized pieces – 1
- Chickpeas drained and rinsed – 15 ounces can
- Pure tomato sauce – 15 ounces can
- Grated ginger, fresh – 1 teaspoon
- Red lentils – ¾ cup

- Turmeric – 1 teaspoon
- Cinnamon – ½ teaspoon
- Cumin – 1 teaspoon
- Salt - ½ teaspoon
- Pepper – ½ teaspoon
- Smoked paprika – 1 teaspoon
- Vegetable broth – 3 cups

To serve:

- Arugula - ¼ cup
- Cooked quinoa - ¼ cup
- Coconut yogurt - ¼ cup

Cooking directions:

1. In a slow cooker and put all the ingredients and combine thoroughly.
2. Cover the cooker and slow cook for 7 hours.
3. Serve it along with arugula, quinoa, and yogurt.

Nutritional value:

Calories: 178 | Total carbohydrate: 37g | Dietary fiber: 11g | Sugars: 8g | Protein: 8g | Sodium: 741mg | Potassium: 986 mg

8. Slow Cooker Spanish Rice

(Perfect Mediterranean Diet recipe)

Preparation: 10 minutes | Cooking: 4 hours 10 minutes | Servings: 8

Ingredients:

- Olive oil – 2 tablespoons, extra olive oil for crockpot greasing.
- Wholegrain rice – 2 cups
- Diced tomatoes in the can – 14½ ounces
- Medium yellow onion, chopped – 1
- Garlic, minced – 3 cloves

- Low-sodium broth or stock (chicken or vegetable), or water – 2 cups
- Red bell pepper, medium cut size – ½
- Yellow bell pepper, medium dice – ½
- Ground cumin – 1 ½ teaspoon
- Chili powder – 2 teaspoons
- Kosher salt – 1½ teaspoons
- Fresh cilantro leaves, for garnishing – 2 tablespoons

Cooking directions:

1. Pour olive oil into a large skillet and bring it to medium heat.
2. Add rice into the skillet and combine well so that the grains get olive oil coating.
3. Now put the onion into the skillet and sauté for about 5 minutes, until the rice becomes pale golden brown.
4. Slightly grease the inside of crockpot with olive oil.
5. Transfer the browned rice to the crockpot.
6. Add broth, bell peppers, tomatoes, garlic, cumin, chili powder, salt and combine thoroughly.
7. Cover the crock, and slow cook for about 4 hours. Two hours later, check if the liquid is being absorbed by the rice well.
8. Continue cooking until the rice becomes soft and all the moisture gets absorbed.
9. Top it with cilantro leaves and serve hot.

Nutritional value:

Calories: 55 | Carbohydrates: 5.36g | Fiber: 1.82g | Protein: 1.01g | Cholesterol: 0g | Sugar: 2.31g | Fat: 3.78g |Sodium: 394.26mg

9. Slow Cooker Turkish/Mediterranean Chickpea Stew

(Perfect Mediterranean Diet recipe)

Preparation: 15 minutes | Cooking: 8 hours 22 minutes | Servings: 7

Ingredients:

- 93% lean ground Turkey – 1.3 pounds package
- Extra virgin olive oil, light – 1 tablespoon
- Poblano pepper, chopped – 3 tablespoons
- Yellow onion, chopped – 1
- Diced carrots – 1 cup
- Garlic cloves, chopped – 2

- Diced celery – 1 cup
- Chickpeas, drained – 30 ounces
- Finely diced tomatoes – 28 ounces can
- Low sodium, 99% fat-free chicken broth – 2 cups
- Paprika – 2 teaspoons
- Turmeric – 2 teaspoons
- Coriander – 1 teaspoon
- Crushed red pepper flakes – ½ teaspoon
- Bay leaves – 2
- Fresh Italian parsley chopped – 2 tablespoons
- Salt – 2 teaspoons
- Cooking spray – as required

Cooking directions:

1. Take a large skillet and spray some non-stick cooking oil in the bottom and bring to medium-high heat.
2. Put ground Turkey in it and cook for about 12 minutes.
3. Break the ground meat into pieces. Mix it well to ensure that it gets cooked uniformly.
4. Transfer the ground meat into the slow cooker.
5. Now in the same skillet pour olive oil and the oil become hot, sauté onions, carrots, pepper, and celery for about 8 minutes until the vegetables become tender and brown.
6. Add garlic in the skillet and sauté for 2 more minutes.
7. Now, transfer the browned vegetables into the slow cooker. Add diced tomatoes, spices, chickpeas and broth as well and mix them lightly.
8. Cover the slow cooker, and set the timer for 8 hours.
9. Remove the bay leaves while serving and top it with fresh herbs.
10. Serve hot.

Nutritional value:

Calories: 342 | Fat: 10g | Cholesterol: 60mg | Sodium: 1081mg | Carbohydrates: 38g | Fiber: 8g | Protein: 24g | Sugar: 3g

10. Whole Wheat Crock Pot Lasagna

(Perfect Mediterranean Diet recipe)

Preparation: 10 minutes | Cooking: 5 hours | Servings: 8

Ingredients:

- Extra lean ground Turkey – 2 pounds
- Uncooked, whole wheat lasagna noodles – 8
- Low fat and low sugar spaghetti sauce – 28 ounces
- Sliced mushrooms – 4 ounces
- Italian seasoning – 1 teaspoon
- Shredded skim milk mozzarella cheese – 2 cups

- Water – ⅓ cup
- Ricotta cheese, fat-free – 15 ounces

Cooking directions:

1. Clean, rinse and drain the mushrooms. Keep them ready.
2. Before starting the cooking, add a little olive oil in the crockpot.
3. Place 4 lasagna noodles in the bottom of the crockpot.
4. In a non-stick pan sauté the ground Turkey until it becomes brown.
5. Add Italian seasoning and mix well.
6. Place half of the browned Turkey over the noodles in the crock pot and spread it well.
7. Spread a layer of ½ of the sauce over Turkey.
8. Now, add another layer of ½ of the mushrooms over it.
9. Similarly, add a layer of ½ of the ricotta and then, half of the mozzarella over it.
10. Repeat the layering.
11. Cover the crock pot and slow cook for 5 hours.

Nutritional value:

Calories: 469 | Total Carbohydrates: 31.3g | Dietary Fiber: 5.2g | Protein: 36.7g | Fat: 21g | Cholesterol: 76.2mg | Sodium: 639.2 mg

CHICKEN

1. Slow Cooker Mediterranean Chicken

(Perfect Mediterranean Diet recipe)

Preparation: 15 minutes | Cooking: 4 hours 30 minutes | Servings: 4

Ingredients:

- Chicken broth, low sodium - 1 cup
- Skinless, boneless chicken breasts - 1 pound
- Juice of lemon – 1
- Sliced onion - 1 medium
- Chopped tomatoes – 2 medium
- Ground pepper - ½ teaspoon
- Black olives - 1/2 cup
- Whole wheat orzo - ¾ cup
- Chopped fresh parsley - 2 tablespoons
- Lemon zest - 4
- Herbes de Provence - 1 teaspoon
- Salt - ½ teaspoon

Cooking directions:

1. Cut the chicken breasts half into four different pieces
2. Combine broth, chicken, onion, tomatoes, lemon juice, lemon zest, salt, herbs de Provence and pepper in a six-quart slow cooker.
3. Cook it on a slow cook mode for 4 hours.
4. Stir in olives and orzo.
5. Cook it further for 30 minutes
6. Let it cool for a few minutes, sprinkle some parsley and serve.

Nutritional values:

Calories: 278 | Carbohydrate: 29g | Protein: 29g | Sugars: 3g |Fat: 5g | Dietary Fiber: 7g | Cholesterol: 63mg | Sodium: 434mg | Potassium: 451mg

2. Slow Cooker Greek Chicken

(Perfect Mediterranean Diet recipe)

Preparation: 20 minutes | Cooking: 3 hours | Servings: 4

Ingredients:

- Skinless, boneless chicken thighs or breasts - 2 pounds
- Extra virgin olive oil - 1 tablespoon
- Ground black pepper - ¼ teaspoon
- Drained and chopped roasted red peppers - 12 ounces
- Red onion, half-inch cut size - 1 medium
- Olives - 1 cup
- Garlic, grated - 1 tablespoon
- Red wine vinegar - 3 tablespoons
- Dried oregano - 1 teaspoon

- Honey - 1 teaspoon
- Dried thyme leaves - 1 teaspoon
- Chopped fresh herbs - thyme or parsley
- Kosher salt - ½ teaspoon
- Feta cheese - ½ cup

Cooking directions:

1. Coat with a little olive oil in a 5-quart slow cooker.
2. Pour olive oil in large skillet and bring to medium-high heat.
3. Season chicken with pepper, and salt.
4. Put the seasoned chicken in the hot skillet.
5. Let the chicken cook for three minutes until it becomes brown on both sides.
6. After browning, transfer the chicken to the five-quart slow cooker.
7. Arrange the olives, onions, and peppers all around the chicken.
8. In a small bowl whisk together garlic, red wine vinegar, oregano, honey, and thyme.
9. Pour the mixture over the vegetables and chicken.
10. Close the lid and slow cook for 4 hours.
11. Garnish with fresh herbs and feta cheese before serving.
12. Serve hot.

Nutritional values:

Calories: 399 | Carbohydrate: 13g | Protein: 50g | Sugars: 9g |Fat: 17g | Dietary Fiber: 2g | Cholesterol: 140mg | Sodium: 1093mg

3. Crock Pot Mediterranean Chicken

(Perfect Mediterranean Diet recipe)

Preparation: 5 minutes | Cooking: 6 hours | Servings: 4

Ingredients:

- Curry powder - 1 tablespoon
- Skinless, boneless chicken breasts - 32 ounces
- Dried thyme - 2 teaspoons
- Dried basil - 2 teaspoons
- Black pepper - 1 teaspoon
- Drained and quartered artichoke hearts, two can - 28 ounces
- Drained and chopped tomatoes, one can - 28 ounces
- Chopped onion - 1 medium

- Low sodium chicken broth - 1 cup
- White wine vinegar - ¼ cup
- Pitted and chopped olives - ½ cup
- Chopped cilantro fresh - ¼ cup
- Kosher salt - 1 teaspoon

Cooking directions:

1. Put chicken breasts in a 6-quart slow cooker.
2. Combine basil, curry powder, thyme, basil, pepper, and salt thoroughly.
3. Season the chicken with half portions of this seasoning mixture.
4. Now, add tomatoes, chicken broth, artichoke hearts, white wine vinegar, olives, and onion into the slow cooker.
5. Add the remaining seasoning mixture into the slow cooker as well.
6. Cover the cooker lid and slow cook for 8 hours.
7. Once it has cooked thoroughly, remove the chicken breasts from the slow cooker.
8. Shred the chicken breasts meat by using forks.
9. Stir in the shredded chicken breasts back to the slow cooker and cook for about 30 minutes.
10. Sprinkle chopped fresh cilantro while serving.

Nutritional values:

Calories: 305 | Carbohydrate: 6g | Protein: 49g | Sugars: 2g |Fat: 8g | Dietary Fiber: 2g | Cholesterol: 129mg | Sodium: 554mg

4. Crock Pot Italian Chicken

(Perfect Mediterranean Diet recipe)

Preparation: 5 minutes | Cooking: 4 hours | Servings: 4

Ingredients:

- Italian dressing seasoning - 1 packet
- Boneless chicken breasts chopped into small pieces - 4
- Cream of chicken soup - 2 cans
- Cream cheese - 8 ounces
- Pasta - 2 cups

Cooking directions:

1. Combine both the cans of soup, Italian dressing seasoning and softened cream cheese together and then transfer it into a crock pot.
2. Place the chicken breast pieces on top of this mix.
3. Cook it on low heat for 4 hours.
4. Boil the pasta as per the directions on the package.
5. Serve it over the pasta.

Nutritional values:

Calories: 388.6 | Carbohydrate: 14.8g | Protein: 51.9g | Fat: 11.1g | Dietary Fiber: 0g | Cholesterol: 118.8mg | Sodium: 1541.3mg

5. Slow Cooker Italian Chicken

(Perfect Mediterranean Diet recipe)

Preparation: 15 minutes | Cooking: 4 hours | Servings: 6

Ingredients:

- Italian dressing - 0.6 ounces
- Skinless, boneless chicken breasts - 4
- Softened cream cheese one can - 8 ounces
- Cream of chicken soup - 10¾ ounces

Cooking directions:

1. Place the chicken breasts into the slow cooker.

2. Sprinkle Italian dressing all over the chicken breasts.
3. Combine cream of chicken soup and cream cheese in a small bowl and cook it under low heat, until it melts down completely.
4. Pour it over the chicken breasts in the slow cooker.
5. Cover the cooker and slow cook for 4 hours.
6. After cooking, take out the chicken and shred it.
7. Add back the shredded chicken into the slow cooker
8. Serve over pasta or rice.

Nutritional values:

Calories: 177 | Carbohydrate: 4.8g | Protein: 5.6g | Sugars: 0.8g |Fat: 15.3g | Dietary Fiber: 0.3g | Cholesterol: 50mg | Sodium: 293mg | Potassium: 84mg

6. Crock Pot Greek Chicken & Salad

(Perfect Mediterranean Diet recipe)

Preparation: 15 minutes | Cooking: 4 hours | Servings: 4

Ingredients:

For the Chicken:

- Skinless chicken thighs with bone - 4 ounces
- Minced garlic - 4 cloves
- Lemon juice – 2 lemon
- Feta cheese, grated - 2 tablespoons
- Dried oregano - 3 teaspoons
- Pepper - ¼ teaspoon
- Salt - ¼ teaspoon

For the Salad:

- Sliced cucumbers - 2 large
- Chopped tomatoes - 4 medium
- Olive oil - 1 tablespoon
- Onion - ½ medium
- Feta cheese, grated - ¼ cup
- White wine vinegar - 1 teaspoon

Cooking directions:

1. Season the chicken thighs with garlic, pepper, salt, and oregano.
2. Place the chicken thighs into the crockpot.
3. Pour the lemon juice all over the chicken thighs.
4. Cover the crock pot and low cook for 4 hours.
5. While the cooking is in progress, you can prepare the salad.
6. Combine cucumbers, onion, and tomatoes in a small bowl.
7. Take another bowl and whisk vinegar and olive oil.
8. Pour this dressing all over the salad mixture.
9. Toss it well and then refrigerate until the chicken is ready to serve.
10. While serving, dress the chicken with the Greek salad on the side.
11. Sprinkle feta cheese on top of chicken.

Nutritional values:

Calories: 301 | Carbohydrate: 18g | Protein: 24g | Sugars: 3g |Fat: 16g | Dietary Fiber: 5g | Cholesterol: 103mg | Sodium: 375mg

7. Slow Coo

(Perfect Me

Preparation: 5 minutes | C

Ingredients:

- Sliced onions - 1 cup
- Olive oil – 2 tablespoons
- Skinless, boneless chicken thighs - 10
- Garlic powder - 2 tablespoons
- Lemon juice - ¼ cup
- Dried oregano - 1 tablespoon
- Smoked paprika - 1 tablespoon
- Salt - ¼ teaspoon

...ions:

1. ...art slow cooker, put chicken thighs and the sliced ...ns.
2. ...ur olive oil and toss it.
3. Add garlic powder, dried oregano, smoked paprika, salt, and lemon juice into the slow cooker.
4. Toss it until they get completely coated with the chicken thighs.
5. Cover the slow cooker and cook on low heat for 4½ hours.
6. Once the chicken is cooked thoroughly, remove it from the slow cooker and shred the meat.
7. Add back the shredded chicken into the slow cooker.
8. Give it a good mix and cook for another 30 minutes.
9. Sprinkle some feta cheese over the chicken before serving.

Nutritional values:

Calories: 400 | Carbohydrate: 7g | Protein: 25g | Sugars: 1g | Fat: 29g | Dietary Fiber: 1g | Cholesterol: 147mg | Sodium: 120mg

8. Crock Pot Turkish Chicken

(Perfect Mediterranean Diet recipe)

Preparation: 5 minutes | Cooking: 8 hours 5 minutes | Servings: 4

Ingredients:

- Green olives - 14 ounces
- Whole chicken - 1
- Tomato paste - 4 ounces
- Bottle beer - 16 ounces
- Pepper - ¼ teaspoon
- Salt - ¼ teaspoon
- Garlic powder - 1 teaspoon
- Paprika chopped - ¼ cup

Cooking directions:

1. Wash the chicken under running tap water and put it in a collator to drain.
2. Now season the drained chicken with pepper, salt, garlic powder, and paprika.
3. Put the chicken into the slow cooker.
4. In a jar combine tomato paste, beer, olives and transfer this into the slow cooker.
5. Make sure to dump the olives on top of the chicken.
6. Cover the crockpot and slow cook for 8 hours.
7. Serve hot.

Nutritional values:

Calories: 174 | Carbohydrate: 19.1g | Protein: 3.8g | Sugars: 4.3g |Fat: 7.8g | Dietary Fiber: 6.1g | Cholesterol: 0mg | Sodium: 926mg

9. Slow Cooker Mediterranean Chicken & Chickpea Soup

(Perfect Mediterranean Diet recipe)

Preparation: 20 minutes | Cooking: 8 hours 20 minutes | Servings: 6

Ingredients:

- Overnight soaked chickpeas - 1½ cups
- Skinless chicken thighs - 2 pounds
- Tomato paste - 2 tablespoons
- Fire roasted, no-salt diced tomatoes - 15 ounces
- Finely chopped yellow onion - 1 large
- Finely chopped garlic - 4 cloves

- Tomato paste - 2 tablespoons
- Ground cumin - 4 teaspoons
- Bay leaf - 1
- Cayenne pepper - ¼ teaspoon
- Paprika - 4 teaspoons
- Ground pepper - ¼ teaspoon
- Artichoke hearts in the can - 14 ounces
- Pitted and halved oil-cured olives - ¼ cup
- Chopped cilantro - ¼ cup
- Water - 4 cups
- Salt - ½ teaspoon

Cooking directions:

1. Drain the soaked chickpeas.
2. Put it into a six-quart slow cooker and pour 4 cups of water.
3. Add tomatoes, onion, tomato paste, bay leaf, garlic, paprika, cumin, ground pepper, and cayenne. Combine it thoroughly.
4. Now, put the chicken thighs into the slow cooker.
5. Close the lid and low cook it for 8 eight hours.
6. After cooking, take out the chicken and shred the meat.
7. Discard the bones and bay leaf.
8. Put the shredded chicken back into the slow cooker and cook for a further 20 minutes.
9. Add olives, artichokes, and salt into the cooker.
10. Stir it thoroughly.
11. Top the soup with chopped cilantro.
12. Serve hot.

Nutritional values:

Calories: 446 | Carbohydrate: 43g | Protein: 34g | Sugars: 9g |Fat: 15g | Cholesterol: 77mg |Sodium: 762mg |Potassium: 609mg

Henry Wilson

10. Basque Chicken Stew

(Perfect Mediterranean Diet recipe)

Preparation: 20 minutes | Cooking: 4 hours | Servings: 8

Ingredients:

- Red potatoes, large cuts - 1½ pounds
- Boneless and skinless chicken thighs, cut into large pieces - 2 pounds
- Sliced red bell pepper - 1 large
- Thinly sliced onion - 1
- Low sodium chicken broth - 1 cup
- Drained and diced tinned tomatoes - 28 ounces
- Chopped fresh thyme - 2 teaspoons
- Minced garlic - 4 cloves
- Ground pepper - ½ teaspoon

- Pimiento-stuffed olives - ½ cup
- Crushed dried savory - ½ teaspoon
- Salt - 1 teaspoon

Cooking directions:

1. Combine potatoes, chicken, bell pepper and onion in a six-quart slow cooker.
2. Stir in the broth, tomatoes, thyme, garlic, pepper, savory and salt.
3. Cover up the slow cooker and slow cook for 8 hours.
4. Stir in the olives into the slow cooker.
5. Serve the stew hot.

Nutritional values:

Calories: 246 | Carbohydrate: 20g | Protein: 23g | Sugars: 4g |Fat: 8g | Dietary Fiber: 3g | Cholesterol: 104mg | Sodium: 685mg | Potassium: 860 mg

MEAT

1. Slow Cooker Mediterranean Beef Roast

Preparation: 10 minutes | Cooking: 10 hours 10 minutes | Servings: 6

Ingredients:

- Chuck roast, boneless - 3 pounds
- Rosemary - 2 teaspoons

- Tomatoes, sun-dried and chopped - ½ cup
- Grated garlic - 10 cloves
- Beef stock - ½ cup
- Balsamic vinegar - 2 tablespoons
- Chopped Italian parsley, fresh - ¼ cup
- Chopped olives - ¼ cup
- Lemon zest - 1 teaspoon
- Cheese grits - ¼ cup

Cooking directions:

1. In the slow cooker, put garlic, sun dried tomatoes, and the beef roast.
2. Add beef stock and Rosemary.
3. Close the cooker and slow cook for 10 hours.
4. After cooking is over, remove the beef, and shred the meet.
5. Discard the fat.
6. Add back the shredded meat to the slow cooker and simmer for 10 minutes.
7. In a small bowl combine lemon zest, parsley, and olives
8. Refrigerate the mixture until you are ready to serve.
9. Garnish using the refrigerated mix.
10. Serve it over pasta or egg noodles.
11. Top it with cheese grits.

Nutritional values:

Calories: 314 | Carbohydrate: 1g | Protein: 32g | Sugars: 0.1g |Fat: 19g | Dietary Fiber: 0.1g | Cholesterol: 91mg | Sodium: 319mg | Potassium: 503mg

2. Slow Cooker Mediterranean Beef with Artichokes

Preparation: 200 minutes | Cooking: 7 hours 8 minutes | Servings: 6

Ingredients:

- Beef for stew - 2 pounds
- Artichoke hearts - 14 ounces
- Grapeseed oil - 1 tablespoon
- Diced onion - 1
- Beef broth – 32 ounces
- Garlic, grated - 4 cloves
- Tinned tomatoes, diced - 14½ ounces
- Tomato sauce - 15 ounces

- Dried oregano - 1 teaspoon
- Pitted, chopped olives - ½ cup
- Dried parsley - 1 teaspoon
- Dried oregano - 1 teaspoon
- Ground cumin - ½ teaspoon
- Dried basil - 1 teaspoon
- Bay leaf – 1
- Salt - ½ teaspoon

Cooking directions:

1. In a large non-stick skillet pour some oil and bring to medium-high heat.
2. Roast the beef until it turns brown on both the sides.
3. Transfer the beef into a slow cooker.
4. Add in beef broth, diced tomatoes, tomato sauce, salt and combine.
5. Pour in beef broth, diced tomatoes, oregano, olives, basil, parsley, bay leaf, and cumin. Combine the mixture thoroughly.
6. Close the slow cooker and cook on low heat for 7 hours.
7. Discard the bay leaf at the time serving.
8. Serve hot.

Nutritional values:

Calories: 416 | Carbohydrate: 14.1g | Protein: 29.9g | Sugars: 5g |Fat: 26.2g | Dietary Fiber: 3.6g | Cholesterol: 83mg | Sodium: 1453mg | Potassium: 745mg

3. Slow Cooker Mediterranean Beef Stew

Preparation: 10 minutes | Cooking: 10 hours | Servings: 10

Ingredients:

- Beef meat (for stew) - 3 pounds
- Beef broth – 2 cups
- Baby mushrooms - 16 ounces
- Garlic, minced - 10 cloves
- Chopped onion - 1 large
- Dried rosemary - 2 tablespoons
- Tomato sauce - 15 ounces
- Balsamic vinegar - ½ cup
- Diced tomatoes in a can - 14½ ounces
- Jar capers, drained - 2 ounces

- Drained black olives - 6
- Salt - ½ teaspoon
- Pepper - ½ teaspoon

For Garnish:

- Parmesan cheese, grated
- Parsley, fresh chopped

Cooking directions:

1. Put all the ingredients except the ingredients for garnishing in a 6-quart slow cooker and combine.
2. Cover the cooker and slow cook for 10 hours.
3. Add pepper and salt as required.
4. Garnish with parmesan and chopped parsley while serving.

Nutritional values:

Calories: 273 | Carbohydrate: 16g | Protein: 33g | Sugars: 6g |Fat: 9g |Sodium: 931mg

...hy Slow Cooker Mediterranean Style Pot Roast

Preparation: 30 minutes | Cooking: 8 hours | Servings: 10

Ingredients:

- Eye of round roast - 4 pounds
- Garlic - 4 cloves
- Olive oil - 2 teaspoons
- Freshly ground black pepper - 1 teaspoon
- Chopped onions - 1 cup
- Carrots, chopped - 4
- Dried Rosemary - 2 teaspoons
- Chopped celery stalks - 2
- Crushed tomatoes in the can - 28 ounces

- Low sodium beef broth - 1 cup
- Red wine - 1 cup
- Salt - 2 teaspoons

Cooking directions:

1. Season the beef roast with salt, garlic, and pepper and set aside.
2. Pour oil in a non-stick skillet and bring to medium-high heat
3. Put the beef into it and roast until it becomes brown on all sides.
4. Now, transfer the roasted beef into a 6-quart slow cooker.
5. Add carrots, onion, rosemary, and celery into the skillet. Continue cooking until the onion and vegetable become soft.
6. Stir in the tomatoes and wine into this vegetable mixture.
7. Add beef broth and tomato mixture into the slow cooker along with the vegetable mixture.
8. Cover the slow cooker and cook on low heat setting for 8 hours.
9. Once the meat gets cooked, remove it from the slow cooker and place it on a cutting board and wrap with an aluminum foil.
10. If you want to thicken the sauce, then transfer it into a saucepan and boil it under low heat for about ten to fifteen minutes until it reaches to the required consistency.
11. Discard fats before serving.

Nutritional values:

Calories: 260 | Carbohydrate: 8.7g | Protein: 37.6g | Fat: 6g | Dietary Fiber: 3g

5. Slow Cooker Meatloaf Recipe

Preparation: 10 minutes | Cooking: 6 hours 10 minutes | Servings: 8

Ingredients:

- Ground bison - 2 pounds
- Grated zucchini - 1
- Eggs – 2 large
- Olive oil cooking spray – as required
- Zucchini, shredded - 1
- Parsley, fresh, finely chopped - ½ cup
- Parmesan cheese, shredded - ½ cup
- Balsamic vinegar - 3 tablespoons
- Garlic, grated - 4 cloves
- Onion minced, dry - 2 tablespoons

- Dried oregano - 1 tablespoon
- Ground black pepper - ½ teaspoon
- Kosher salt - ½ teaspoon

For the topping:

- Shredded mozzarella cheese - ¼ cup
- Ketchup without sugar - ¼ cup
- Freshly chopped parsley - ¼ cup

Cooking directions:

1. Stripe line the inside of a six-quart slow cooker with aluminum foil.
2. Spray non-stick cooking oil over it.
3. In a large bowl combine ground bison or extra lean ground sirloin, zucchini, eggs, parsley, balsamic vinegar, garlic, dried oregano, sea or kosher salt, minced dry onion, and ground black pepper.
4. Transfer this mixture into the slow cooker and form an oblong shaped loaf.
5. Cover the cooker, set on a low heat and cook for 6 hours.
6. After cooking, open the cooker and spread ketchup all over the meatloaf.
7. Now, place the cheese above the ketchup as a new layer and close the slow cooker.
8. Let the meatloaf sit on these two layers for about 10 minutes or until the cheese starts to melt.
9. Garnish with fresh parsley, and shredded mozzarella cheese.

Henry Wilson

Nutritional values:

Calories: 320 | Carbohydrate: 4g | Protein: 26g | Sugars: 2g |Fat: 20g | Dietary Fiber: 1g | Cholesterol: 131mg | Sodium: 403mg | Potassium: 507mg

6. Slow Cooker Mediterranean Beef Hoagies

Preparation: 10 minutes | Cooking: 13 hours | Servings: 6

Ingredients:

- Beef top round roast fatless - 3 pounds
- Onion powder - ½ teaspoon
- Black pepper - ½ teaspoon
- Low sodium beef broth - 3 cups
- Salad dressing mix - 4 teaspoons
- Bay leaf - 1
- Garlic, minced - 1 tablespoon
- Red bell peppers, thin strips cut - 2
- Pepperoncino - 16 ounces
- Sargento Provolone, thin - 8 slices
- Gluten-free bread - 2 ounces
- Salt - ½ teaspoon

Henry Wilson

For seasoning:

- Onion powder - 1½ tablespoon
- Garlic powder - 1½ tablespoon
- Dried parsley - 2 tablespoon
- Stevia - 1 tablespoon
- Dried thyme - ½ teaspoon
- Dried oregano - 1 tablespoon
- Black pepper - 2 tablespoons
- Salt - 1 tablespoon
- Cheese slice - 6

Cooking directions:

1. Pat dry the roast with a paper towel.
2. Combine black pepper, onion powder and salt in a small bowl and rub the mixture over the roast.
3. Place the seasoned roast into a slow cooker.
4. Add broth, salad dressing mix, bay leaf, and garlic to the slow cooker. Combine it gently.
5. Cover the slow cooker and set to low cooking for 12 hours.
6. After cooking, remove the bay leaf.
7. Take out the cooked beef and shred the beef meet.
8. Put back the shredded beef and add bell peppers and
9. Add bell peppers and pepperoncino into the slow cooker.
10. Cover the cooker and low cook for 1 hour.
11. Before serving, top each of the bread with 3 ounces of the meat mixture.
12. Top it with a cheese slice.
13. The liquid gravy can be used as a dip.

Nutritional values:

Calories: 442 | Carbohydrate: 37g | Protein: 49g | Sugars: 3.5g | Fat: 11.5g | Dietary Fiber: 4g | Cholesterol: 116mg | Sodium: 873mg

7. Mediterranean Pork Roast

Preparation: 10 minutes | Cooking: 8 hours 10 minutes | Servings: 6

Ingredients:

- Olive oil - 2 tablespoons
- Pork roast - 2 pounds
- Paprika - ½ teaspoon
- Chicken broth - ¾ cup
- Dried sage - 2 teaspoons
- Garlic minced - ½ tablespoon
- Dried marjoram - ¼ teaspoon

- Dried Rosemary - ¼ teaspoon
- Oregano - 1 teaspoon
- Dried thyme - ¼ teaspoon
- Basil - 1 teaspoon
- Kosher salt - ½ teaspoon

Cooking directions:

1. In a small bowl mix broth, oil, salt, and spices.
2. In a skillet pour olive oil and bring to medium-high heat.
3. Put the pork into it and roast until all sides become brown.
4. Take out the pork after cooking and poke the roast all over with a knife.
5. Place the poked pork roast into a 6-quart crock pot.
6. Now, pour the small bowl mixture liquid all over the roast.
7. Close the crock pot and cook on low heat setting for 8 hours.
8. After cooking, remove it from the crock pot on to a cutting board and shred into pieces.
9. Afterward, add the shredded pork back into the crockpot.
10. Simmer it another 10 minutes.
11. Serve along with feta cheese, pita bread, and tomatoes.

Nutritional values:

Calories: 361 | Carbohydrate: 0.7g | Protein: 43.8g | Sugars: 0.1g |Fat: 10.4g | Dietary Fiber: 0.3g | Cholesterol: 130mg | Sodium: 374mg |Potassium: 647mg

8. Pulled Pork with Bourbon-Peach Barbecue Sauce

Preparation: 30 minutes | Cooking: 7 hours | Servings: 12

Ingredients:

- Pork with bone, trimmed, shoulder roast - 3½ pounds
- Spanish smoked paprika - 2 teaspoons
- Ground black pepper, fresh - 1 teaspoon
- Chicken stock, unsalted - ½ cup
- Molasses - ⅓ cup
- Balsamic vinegar - ⅓ cup
- Crushed red pepper - 1 teaspoon
- Soy sauce, low sodium - 2 teaspoons
- Onion, vertically sliced - 2 cups
- Peach preserves - ½ cup

- Bourbon - ¼ cup
- Kosher salt - 1¼ teaspoons
- Olive oil – as required
- Garlic, minced - 5 cloves
- Cornstarch - 2 teaspoons
- Cold water - 2 tablespoons

Cooking directions:

1. Combine salt, black pepper, and paprika in a small bowl.
2. Apply this mixture all over the pork.
3. Take a large skillet and coat some cooking spray and bring to medium-high heat.
4. Add the pork to the pan and cook it for 10 minutes until it turns brown on both sides.
5. Once the pork gets brown, transfer it into a 6-quart slow cooker.
6. Add the stock, molasses, balsamic vinegar, red pepper, and low sodium soy sauce into the skillet. Boil these ingredients.
7. Pour this mixture all over the pork in the slow cooker.
8. Top it up with garlic and onion.
9. Cover the slow cooker and low cook for 6½ hours.
10. Once the pork is wholly cooked, transfer it to a cutting board and shred.
11. Remove onion from the slow cooker and add it to the pork
12. Take a large 4-cup measuring cup glass and place a large sized top open zip plastic bag into it.
13. Pour the cooking liquid into the bag.
14. Let the liquid stand in the bag for about ten minutes so that the fat rises to the top.
15. Seal the bag and carefully prick the bottom corner of the bag and let the liquid drip into the skillet until the fat layer reaches the prickled opening.
16. Stop dripping and discard fat.

17. Whisk the bourbon with the liquid and boil.
18. Boil for 10 minutes or until the mixture reduces to 1½ cup.
19. Now, combine cornstarch and cold water in a separate small bowl.
20. Whisk it and then add it to the sauce.
21. Keep stirring it constantly until it turns into a thick consistency.
22. Stir in the remaining salt.
23. Drizzle the sauce all over the pork and toss it for an even coating.

Nutritional values:

Calories: 267 | Carbohydrate: 19g | Protein: 35.1g | Fat: 4.8g | Dietary Fiber: 0.8g | Sugars: 12.4g | Cholesterol: 97mg | Sodium: 161mg

9. Beef Stew with Rosemary & Balsamic Vinegar

Preparation: 25 minutes | Cooking: 8 hours | Servings: 6

Ingredients:

- Sliced mushrooms - 8 ounces
- Olive oil - 2 tablespoons
- Diced chuck steak - 2 pounds
- Diced onion - 1
- Tomatoes with juice, diced - 14½ ounces
- Beef stock - 1 cup
- Balsamic vinegar - ¼ cup
- Tomato sauce - ½ cup
- Garlic, coarsely chopped - ½ cup

- Half cut black olives – 2 cups
- Fresh parsley, finely chopped - 2 tablespoons
- Rosemary, fresh, chopped - 2 tablespoons
- Salt - ½ teaspoon
- Fresh ground black pepper - ½ teaspoon
- Capers - 1 tablespoon

Cooking directions:

1. Pour some olive oil in a non-stick pan and bring to medium-high temperature.
2. Add mushrooms to the pan and cook for 8 minutes or until the mushrooms become brown and transfer the roasted mushrooms into the slow cooker.
3. Add some more oil to the pan and cook the diced onions for 5 minutes or until it becomes brown. Transfer the cooked onion also to the slow cooker.
4. Again pour some oil into the pan and put the diced beef.
5. Continue cooking until the beef becomes brown and transfer the roasted beef to the slow cooker.
6. Now pour a cup of beef stock into the pan and simmer on low heat. Scrap off the food items stuck to the pan and transfer the liquid to the slow cooker.
7. Add tomato sauce, diced tomatoes with juice, olives, balsamic vinegar, rosemary, garlic, capers, black pepper and parsley to the slow cooker and combine it thoroughly.
8. Close the slow cooker and cook on low heat for 8 hours.
9. After cooking, season the beef with freshly grounded black pepper and salt.

Nutritional values:

Calories: 529 | Carbohydrate: 14.5g | Protein: 50.8g | Sugars: 4.9g | Fat: 29.8g | Dietary Fiber: 3.6g | Cholesterol: 160mg | Sodium: 802mg | Potassium: 860mg

10. Plum Pork Tenderloin

Preparation: 10 minutes | Cooking: 6 hours | Servings: 3

Ingredients:

- Trimmed pork tenderloins - 1 pound
- Ground allspice - 1 tablespoon
- Ground cinnamon - 1 tablespoon
- Olive oil – as required
- Water - ½ cup
- Plum sauce - 9.3 ounces
- Plums cut into 6 wedges – 2 plum

Cooking directions:

1. Combine allspice and cinnamon in a small bowl.
2. Season the pork by rubbing the allspice mix over it.
3. Coat a 5-quart slow cooker with little cooking spray and place the pork into it.
4. Pour the plum sauce and plums over the pork.
5. Add half a cup of water and the plum wedges to the slow cooker.
6. Cover the cooker and slow cook for 8 hours.
7. Serve hot.

Nutritional values:

Calories: 199 | Carbohydrate: 17.6g | Protein: 24.3g | Fat: 2.9g | Dietary Fiber: 1.3g | Cholesterol: 74mg | Sodium: 238mg | Calcium: 23mg | Iron: 1.7mg

Fish & Seafood

1. Slow Cooker Mediterranean Salmon

(Perfect Mediterranean Diet recipe)

Preparation: 10 minutes | Cooking: 6 hours | Servings: 4

Ingredients:

- Salmon fillets - 1 pound
- Italian seasoning - 1 tablespoon
- Onion powder - 1 teaspoon
- Garlic powder - 1 teaspoon
- Olive oil - 1 tablespoon
- Black pepper - ½ teaspoon
- Onion, nicely chopped - ½
- Garlic, minced - 3 cloves
- Red bell pepper - 1
- Quartered and sliced zucchini - 1
- Chopped tomato – 1
- Olive oil – as required

Cooking directions:

1. Take an oven safe-dish that fits perfectly inside a six-quart slow cooker.
2. Spray some cooking oil inside the oven safe dish.
3. In a medium bowl put half portion of the garlic powder, Italian seasoning, onion powder, olive oil, and black pepper. Combine the ingredients thoroughly.
4. Add the sliced garlic cloves, zucchini, onions, tomato, and bell pepper as well
5. Season the salmon fillets with the mix and place the fillets one by one into the bottom part of the oven-safe dish.
6. Season it with the remaining herbs, olive oil, and spices.
7. Gently toss it up with the vegetables to coat them thoroughly.
8. Cover up the oven-safe dish using a glass lid.
9. Place the dish correctly inside the slow cooker and cover the cooker.
10. Now low cook it for six hours.

11. Serve it with couscous or whole grain pasta.

Nutritional values:

Calories: 225 | Carbohydrate: 8.1g | Protein: 23.5g | Sugars: 4.1g |Fat: 11.8g | Dietary Fiber: 1.6g | Cholesterol: 52mg | Sodium: 59mg | Potassium: 704mg

2. Mediterranean Shrimp Soup

(Perfect Mediterranean Diet recipe)

Preparation: 15 minutes | Cooking: 5 hours | Servings: 6

Ingredients:

- Peeled, veined, uncooked medium shrimp - 1 pound
- Diced tomatoes - 14 ounces
- Chicken broth, low sodium - 14 ounces
- Chopped onion - 1 medium
- Tomato sauce - 8 ounces
- Orange juice - ½ cup
- Bell pepper, green, chopped - 1 medium
- Sliced mushrooms - 2½ ounces
- Dry white wine (optional) - ½ cup

- Garlic, minced - 2 cloves
- Sliced ripe olives - ¼ cup
- Bay leaves - 2
- Dried basil - 1 teaspoon
- Crushed fennel seeds - ¼ teaspoon
- Black pepper - ¼ teaspoon

Cooking directions:

1. In a slow cooker and add diced tomatoes, reduced sodium chicken broth, chopped onion, tomato sauce, orange juice, chopped green bell pepper, dry white wine, orange juice, sliced ripe olives, sliced mushrooms, bay leaves, dried basil, minced garlic, black pepper, and crushed fennel seeds. Combine the ingredients thoroughly.
2. Cover the slow cooker and slow cook for 4½ hours until the vegetables become tender.
3. Afterward, stir in the shrimp into the slow cooker.
4. Cover the cooker and again slow cook for 30 minutes.
5. Discard the bay leaves before serving.

Nutritional values:

Calories: 162 | Carbohydrate: 12g | Protein: 21g | Fat: 3g | Dietary Fiber: 2g | Cholesterol: 129mg | Sodium: 678mg

3. Slow Cooker Seafood Stew

(Perfect Mediterranean Diet recipe)

Preparation: 20 minutes | Cooking: 5 hours 5 minutes| Servings: 8

Ingredients:

- Whitefish, cut to 1" size – 1 pound
- Shrimp, medium, shelled, uncooked, veined - ¾ pound
- Tined crab meat, drained – 6 ounces.
- Onions, sliced - 2 cups
- Tinned tomatoes, diced with liquid - 28 ounces
- Garlic, grated - 5 cloves
- Tomato paste - 6 ounces

- Clam juice - 8 ounces
- Red wine vinegar - 1 tablespoon
- Dry white wine - ½ cup
- Dried Italian seasoning - 2½ teaspoons
- Olive oil - 1 tablespoon
- Crushed red pepper flakes - ¼ teaspoon
- Sugar - ¼ teaspoon
- Celery finely chopped - 2 stalks
- Bay leaf - 1
- Chopped clams with juice - 6½ ounces
- Chopped fresh parsley - 1/4 cup

Cooking directions:

1. Combine celery, onions, clam juice, tomatoes, wine, tomato paste, Italian seasoning, vinegar, pepper flakes, bay leaf, and sugar in a 6-quart slow cooker.
2. Close the slow cooker and cook on low heat for 8 hours.
3. Stir in shrimp, fish, crabmeat, and clams with juice into the stew.
4. Continue slow cooking for 2 hours.
5. Remove the bay leaf before serving.
6. For seasoning, stir in parsley.
7. Serve hot.

Nutritional values:

Calories: 215 | Carbohydrate: 15g | Protein: 30g | Sugars: 5g |Fat: 4g | Dietary Fiber: 3g | Cholesterol: 125mg | Sodium: 610mg

4. Slow Cooker Spanish Shrimp Stew

(Perfect Mediterranean Diet recipe)

Preparation: 10 minutes | Cooking: 3½ hours | Servings: 4

Ingredients:

- Frozen shrimp - 10 ounces
- Vegetable broth - 2 cups
- Rinsed quinoa - 1 cup
- Olive oil - 1 tablespoon
- Tomatoes, tinned, fire roasted, drained – 14 ounces
- Lime juice - 1 tablespoon
- Honey - 2 tablespoons
- Cayenne pepper - ½ teaspoon
- Worcestershire sauce - 1 tablespoon
- Onion powder - 1 teaspoon

- Smoked paprika - ½ teaspoon
- Frozen spinach - 1 cup
- Dried coriander - 1 teaspoon
- Pepper ground - ½ teaspoon
- Goat cheese, shredded - 1 cup
- Chopped green onion - 1 cup
- Salt - ½ teaspoon
- Fresh parsley, chopped - 1 cup
- Olive oil – as required

Cooking directions:

1. Grease the crockpot using cooking spray
2. Add in broth, quinoa, olive oil, tomatoes, lime juice, honey, cayenne, Worcestershire sauce, onion powder, paprika, spinach, coriander, and shrimp.
3. Stir to combine all these ingredients.
4. Close the crockpot and slow cook for 3½ hours.
5. Season it with pepper and salt.
6. Garnish with goat cheese, green onions, and parsley.

Nutritional values:

Calories: 345 | Carbohydrate: 47g | Protein: 23g | Sugars: 13g |Fat: 7g | Dietary Fiber: 5g | Cholesterol: 178mg | Sodium: 1251mg |Potassium: 533mg

5. Crock Pot Seafood Stew

(Perfect Mediterranean Diet recipe)

Preparation: 10 minutes | Cooking: 7 hours | Servings: 6

Ingredients:

- Crab legs, extra-large shrimp and scallops, thawed - 2 pounds
- Vegetable broth - 4 cups
- Crushed tomatoes - 28 ounces
- Garlic, grated - 3 cloves
- White wine - ½ cup
- Diced onion - ½ cup

- Baby potatoes - 1 pound
- Dried basil - 1 teaspoon
- Dried thyme - 1 teaspoon
- Celery salt - ½ teaspoon
- Dried cilantro - 1 teaspoon
- Pepper ground - ½ teaspoon
- Salt - ½ teaspoon
- Cayenne pepper - ¼ teaspoon
- Red pepper flakes - ¼ teaspoon

Cooking directions:

1. Excluding the thawed seafood, put all the ingredients in a 6-quart slow cooker and combine thoroughly.
2. Close the slow cooker and cook on low heat for 6 hours.
3. After 6 hours, add the thawed seafood and cook for 1 hour on high heat.
4. Serve hot.

Nutritional values:

Calories: 236 | Carbohydrate: 31g | Protein: 22g | Sugars: 8g |Fat: 1g | Dietary Fiber: 4g | Cholesterol: 36mg | Sodium: 1789mg | Potassium: 1049mg

6. Slow Cooker Salmon Risotto

(Perfect Mediterranean Diet recipe)

Preparation: 20 minutes | Cooking: 1-hour | Servings: 4

Ingredients:

- Salmon fillet, skinned and diced - 17.63 ounces
- Chopped shallots - 2
- Olive oil - 2 tablespoons
- Vegetable broth - 3 cups
- Arborio rice - 1¼ cup
- Diced cucumbers - ½ cup

Henry Wilson

- White wine - 1/2 cup
- Salt - ½ teaspoon
- Chopped green onions - 1
- Pepper - ½ teaspoon

Cooking directions:

1. Pour olive oil into a non-stick pan and bring to medium-high heat.
2. Add cucumber and shallots to the pan and sauté it for about two to three minutes by stirring.
3. Cover the pan and cook on a low heat for 15 minutes.
4. Turn the heat to high and add the rice grains to the pan.
5. Sauté it for one minute by stirring.
6. Afterward, transfer it to a slow cooker.
7. Stir in the wine and the hot broth.
8. Close the slow cooker and cook on low heat for 45 minutes.
9. After 45 minutes, open the cooker and add salmon pieces.
10. Season it with salt and pepper.
11. Cover the cooker and cook further 15 minutes.
12. Once the rice and salmon cooked well, turn off the slow cooker.
13. Let it rest for 5 minutes and stir in green onion and dill.
14. Serve hot.

Nutritional values:

Calories: 320 | Carbohydrate: 41g | Protein: 25g | Sugars: 0g |Fat: 7g | Dietary Fiber: 1g | Cholesterol: 30mg | Sodium: 80.0mg

7. Slow Cooker Mediterranean Shrimp Soup

(Perfect Mediterranean Diet recipe)

Preparation: 10 minutes | Cooking: 5 hours | Servings: 6

Ingredients:

- Peeled shrimp - 1 pound
- Green bell pepper, chopped - ½ medium
- Chopped onion - 1 medium

- Tinned tomatoes, undrained and coarsely chopped - 14½ ounces
- Garlic, minced - 2 cloves
- Tomato sauce - 8 ounces
- Chicken broth with low sodium - 14½ ounces
- Orange juice - 1/2 cup
- Sliced mushrooms - 2½ ounces
- Sliced ripe olives - ¼ cup
- Dry white wine - ½ cup
- Dried basil leaves - 1 teaspoon
- Bay leaves - 2
- Black pepper, ground - ¼ teaspoon
- Crushed fennel seed - ¼ teaspoon

Cooking directions:

1. Excluding shrimp, combine all ingredients in a slow cooker.
2. Close the slow cooker and slow cook for 4½ hours.
3. After cooking add the shrimp and stir.
4. Close the slow cooker and cook for 30 minutes.
5. Discard the bay leaves before serving.

Nutritional values:

Calories: 117 | Carbohydrate: 7g | Protein: 14.4g | Sugars: 6.8g |Fat: 1g | Dietary Fiber: 2.4g | Cholesterol: 81mg | Sodium: 475mg |Potassium: 451mg

8. Hearty Crock Pot Shrimp Stew

(Perfect Mediterranean Diet recipe)

Preparation: 30 minutes | Cooking: 8 hours Servings: 6

Ingredients:

- Catfish cut into 2" sized pieces - 1½ pounds
- Olive oil - 2 tablespoons
- Onion sliced - 1 large
- Garlic minced - 1 large clove
- Zucchini squash, sliced - 2
- Green bell pepper - 1
- Basil leaf dried - ½ teaspoon

- Tinned tomatoes whole - 14½ ounces
- Salt - 1 teaspoon
- Dried leaf oregano - ½ teaspoon
- Dry white wine - ¼ cup
- Pepper - ⅛ teaspoon
- Sliced mushrooms - 4 ounces

For Garnish:

- Parsley, chopped - ¼ cup

Cooking directions:

1. Put all the ingredients in a 6-quart crockpot and combine it gently.
2. Close the cooker and cook on low heat for 8 hours.
3. While serving, garnish with chopped parsley.

Nutritional values:

Calories: 225 | Carbohydrate: 17g | Protein: 21g |Fat: 8g | Dietary Fiber: 3g | Sodium: 465mg | Cholesterol: 64mg | Calcium: 101mg

9. Mediterranean Cod with Pepper & Tomato

(Perfect Mediterranean Diet recipe)

Preparation: 15 minutes | Cooking: 3 hours 45 minutes|
Servings: 2

Ingredients:

- Cod fillet, boneless, skinless in 5cm cut size - ½ pound
- Sliced red peppers - 2
- Olive oil - 2 teaspoons
- Tinned cherry tomatoes – 14 ounces
- Sliced garlic - 2 cloves
- Basil - ½ ounce
- Sprigs - 2 tablespoons

- Sherry vinegar - 1 teaspoon
- Roughly chopped green olives - ¼ cup
- Rinsed and drained capers - 2 teaspoons
- Ciabatta shredded into pieces - 1¾ ounces

Cooking directions:

1. In a slow cooker pour one teaspoon of olive oil and bring to medium-high heat.
2. Once the oil starts to sizzle, fry the peppers for 10 minutes or until the peppers turn soft.
3. Add garlic to the slow cooker and fry it for a minute.
4. Later on, add sherry vinegar, tomatoes, and basil sprigs.
5. Bring these ingredients to a boil.
6. Close slow cooker and cook on low heat for 3 hours. Check the sauce consistency and maintain as you required.
7. After cooking, remove the basil sprigs.
8. Stir in the olives, capers and the fillet.
9. Let it simmer for 30 minutes on low heat.
10. Now, using a food processor quick stir the chopped basil and ciabatta.
11. Fry the whizzed mixture in a non-stick pan in one teaspoon olive oil.
12. Scatter the toasted bread mixture over the fish before serving.
13. Garnish with chopped basil.

Nutritional values:

Calories: 164 | Carbohydrate: 25.2g | Protein: 5.3g | Sugars: 8.3g |Fat: 6g | Dietary Fiber: 4g | Cholesterol: 0mg | Sodium: 262mg |Potassium: 666mg

10. Mediterranean Seafood Stew

(Perfect Mediterranean Diet recipe)

Preparation: 20 minutes | Cooking: 5½ hours | Servings: 8

Ingredients:

- Shrimp, veined, peeled – 1 pound
- Haddock fillets, 1"cut size – 1 pound
- Tinned crabmeat, drained – 6 ounces
- Tinned clams, chopped, undrained – 6 ounces
- Tinned tomatoes, diced – 28 ounces
- Celery ribs, shredded – 3
- Onions, sliced – 2 medium

- Tomato paste – 6 ounces
- Bottled clam juice – 8 ounces
- Vegetable broth - ½ cup
- Garlic, minced – 5 cloves
- Olive oil – 1 tablespoon
- Red wine vinegar – 1 tablespoon
- Italian seasoning – 2 tablespoons
- Sugar - ½ teaspoon
- Bay leaf -1
- Parsley, finely chopped – 2 tablespoons

Cooking directions:

1. Combine all the ingredients except shrimp, haddock, crabmeat, clams and parsley in a 6-quart slow cooker.
2. Cover the lid and slow cook for 5 hours.
3. Add all the seafood, cover and cook for 30 minutes.
4. Discard bay leaf at the time of serving.
5. Garnish with parsley.

Nutritional values:

Calories: 205 | Carbohydrate: 15g | Protein: 29g | Sugars: 8g |Fat: 3g | Dietary Fiber: 3g | Cholesterol: 125mg | Sodium: 483mg

Mediterranean Desserts

1. Mediterranean Slow Cooker Apple Olive Cake

(Perfect Mediterranean Diet recipe)

Preparation: 20 minutes | Cooking: 2 hours | Servings: 4

Henry Wilson

Ingredients:

- Peeled and chopped Gala apples - 2 large
- Ground cinnamon - ½ teaspoon
- Whole wheat flour - 3 cups
- Orange juice – 2 cups
- Baking powder - 1 teaspoon
- Ground nutmeg - ½ teaspoon
- Sugar - 1 cup
- Baking soda - 1 teaspoon
- Large eggs - 2
- Extra virgin olive oil - 1 cup
- Gold raisins, soaked and drained - ⅔ cup
- Confectioner's sugar - for dusting purpose

Cooking directions:

1. In a small bowl, soak the gold raisins in lukewarm water for 15 minutes and drain. Keep aside.
2. Put the chopped apple in a medium bowl and pour orange juice over it.
3. Toss and make sure the apple gets well coated with the orange juice
4. Combine cinnamon, flour, baking powder, nutmeg in a large bowl and keep aside.
5. Add extra virgin olive oil and sugar into the mixture and combine thoroughly.
6. This particular mixture must be thicker in texture and not a runny one.
7. In the large bowl that contains the dry ingredients, make a circular path in the middle part of the flour mixture
8. Add the olive oil and sugar mixture into this path
9. Make use of a wooden spoon and stir them well until they blend well with one another

10. It must be a thick batter.
11. Drain the excess juice from the apples.
12. Add the apples and raisins to the batter and mix it with a spoon to combine.
13. Once again, the batter must be reasonably thick in terms of texture.
14. In a six quart slow cooker, place a parchment paper and add the batter over it.
15. Turn the heat setting to low and the timer to two hours or cook until the cake does not have any wet spots over it
16. Once the cake has cooked well, wait until the cake cools down before cutting them into pieces
17. Transfer the cake to a serving dish and sprinkle confectioner's sugar on top.

Nutritional values:

Calories: 294 | Carbohydrate: 47.7g | Protein: 5.3g | Sugars: 23.5g |Fat: 11g | Dietary Fiber: 4.3g

2. Mediterranean Crockpot Strawberry Basil Cobbler

(Perfect Mediterranean Diet recipe)

Preparation: 20 minutes | Cooking: 2½ hours | Servings: 5

Ingredients:

- Divided granulated sugar - 1¼ cups
- Divided whole wheat flour - 2½ cups
- Ground cinnamon - ½ teaspoon
- Baking powder - 2 teaspoons
- Skim milk - ½ cup
- Eggs - 2
- Divided salt - ¼ teaspoon

- Canola oil - 4 tablespoons
- Rolled oats - ¼ cup
- Frozen strawberries - 6 cups
- Vanilla frozen yogurt – 3 cups
- Chopped fresh basil - ¼ cup
- Cooking spray – as required

Cooking directions:

1. Combine sugar, flour, baking powder, salt and cinnamon in a large bowl.
2. Add milk, oil, and eggs into the bowl and combine thoroughly.
3. Coat some olive oil in the bottom of the slow cooker.
4. Transfer and spread the mixed batter evenly into the slow cooker.
5. Take another large bowl and combine flour, salt, and sugar.
6. Add basil and strawberries to the bowl and toss it to coat.
7. Pour this mixture on the top of the batter in the slow cooker.
8. Top up with the rolled oat mixture.
9. Close the slow cooker and cook on high heat setting for 2½ hours. You can check the cooking status by inserting a toothpick. If it comes out clean, your cake is ready.
10. Serve topped with frozen vanilla yogurt and basil.

Nutritional values:

Calories: 727 | Carbohydrate: 126.8g | Sugars: 70.4g | Fat: 16.2g | Dietary Fiber: 5.9g | Cholesterol: 75mg | Sodium: 262mg | Protein: 19.6g | Potassium: 962mg

3. Slow Cooker Mediterranean Pumpkin Pecan Bread Pudding

Preparation: 15 minutes | Cooking: 4 hours | Servings: 3

Ingredients:

- Chopped toasted pecans - ½ cup
- Day old whole wheat bread cubes - 8 cups
- Eggs - 4
- Cinnamon chips - ½ cup
- Half n half - 1 cup
- Canned pumpkin - 1 cup
- Melted butter - ½ cup

- Brown sugar - ½ cup
- Cinnamon - ½ teaspoon
- Vanilla - 1 teaspoon
- Ground ginger - ¼ teaspoon
- Nutmeg - ½ teaspoon
- Vanilla ice cream - ¼ cup
- Ground cloves - ⅛ teaspoon
- Caramel ice cream topping - ¼ cup

Cooking directions:

1. Grease a 6-quart crock pot and put the bread cubes, cinnamon, and chopped pecans into it.
2. In a medium bowl, whisk together pumpkin, eggs, brown sugar, half-n-half, vanilla, melted butter, nutmeg, cinnamon, cloves, ginger and pour the mixture over the bread cubes.
3. Stir the mix gently.
4. Cover up the slow cooker and cook for 4 hours. It will be well prepared within 4 hours, which you can check by inserting a toothpick and if it comes clean, it is ready to serve.
5. Before serving, top up with caramel ice cream and vanilla ice cream.

Nutritional values:

Calories: 289 | Carbohydrate: 28g | Protein: 6g | Sugars: 14g | Cholesterol: 83mg | Fat: 17g | Dietary Fiber: 1g | Sodium: 216 mg | Potassium: 166mg

4. Slow Cooker Chocolate Fondue

Preparation: 15 minutes | Cooking: 2 hours | Servings: 3

Ingredients:

- Chocolate Almonds candy bars - 4½ ounces
- Butter - 1½ tablespoons
- Milk - 3 tablespoons
- Miniature marshmallows - 1½ cup
- Heavy whipping cream - ½ cup

Cooking directions:

1. Grease a 2-quart slow cooker and put chocolate, butter, milk, marshmallows into it.

2. Close the cooker and cook on low heat setting for 1½ hours.
3. Stir the mix every 30 minutes to melt and mix whipping cream gradually.
4. After adding whipping cream allow it to settle for 2 hours.
5. Use it as a chocolate dip.

Nutritional values:

Calories: 463 | Carbohydrate: 3901g | Protein: 5.5g | Sugars: 29.4g | Fat: 31.8g | Dietary Fiber: 4.5g | Cholesterol: 39mg | Sodium: 138mg | Potassium: 30mg

5. Chocolate Orange Volcano Pudding

Preparation: 20 minutes | Cooking: 2 hours | Servings: 6

Ingredients:

- Self-raising flour – ½ pound
- Melted butter - 3½ ounces
- Sifted cocoa - 2¾ ounces
- Caster sugar - 5¼ ounces
- Zest and juice of orange - 1
- Baking powder - 1 teaspoon
- Orange flavored milk chocolate, chopped into chunks - 5¼ ounces
- Milk - 1½ cup
- Salt – a pinch

- Water – 2 cups

For the Sauce:

- Cocoa – 1 ounce
- Light brown soft sugar - 7½ ounces

Topping:

- Vanilla ice cream - ¼ cup
- Orange wedges – 1 orange
- Cream - ¼ cup

Cooking directions:

1. Grease the slow cooker with butter.
2. Combine the caster sugar, flour, baking powder, and cocoa, pinch of salt and orange zest in a large mixing bowl thoroughly.
3. Whisk the eggs, orange juice, milk and buttermilk in a medium bowl.
4. Add it to the dry ingredients and combine to form a smooth mixture.
5. Stir in chocolate pieces and then transfer the mixture into the slow cooker
6. Prepare the sauce by mixing cocoa and sugar in two cups of boiling water.
7. Pour the sauce over the pudding mixture.
8. Cover the slow cooker and cook on high heat for two hours.
9. Before serving, top the pudding with vanilla ice cream or cream and orange wedges.

Henry Wilson

Nutritional values:

Calories: 733 | Carbohydrate: 120.8g | Protein: 11.8g | Sugars: 79.3g | Fat: 25.4g | Dietary Fiber: 8.3g | Cholesterol: 48mg | Sodium: 259mg | Potassium: 607mg

6. Slow Cooker Nutella Fudge

Preparation: 10 minutes | Cooking: 1½ minutes | Servings: 5

Ingredients:

- Vanilla essence - 1 teaspoon
- Condensed milk – 14 ounces
- 70 percent dark chocolate - 7 ounces
- Nutella - 1 cup
- Chopped toasted hazelnuts - 4 ounces
- Icing sugar - 3 ounces

Cooking directions:

1. In a slow cooker add vanilla essence, condensed milk, dark chocolate, and Nutella.
2. Cook it for 1½ hours without covering the lid.
3. Make sure to stir the ingredients every ten minutes until they melt completely.
4. After cooking turn off the slow cooker and transfer its content into a large sized mixing bowl
5. Stir in the sieved icing sugar.
6. Take the warm fudge and carefully scrape it flat and allow it cool.
7. Sprinkle the hazelnuts over the fudge and slightly press them downwards, so that they get attached well.
8. Refrigerate this well for 4 hours and then cut them into squares.

Nutritional Value: (Per One Serving)

Calories: 191 | Carbohydrate: 24.7g | Protein: 3.2g | Sugars: 22.4g | Fat: 9.3g | Dietary Fiber: 1.4g | Cholesterol: 5mg | Sodium: 25mg

7. Greek Yogurt Chocolate Mousse

(Perfect Mediterranean Diet recipe)

Preparation: 5 minutes | Cooking: 2 hours | Servings: 4

Ingredients:

- Dark chocolate - 3½ ounces
- Milk - ¾ cup
- Maple syrup - 1 tablespoon
- Greek yogurt - 2 cups
- Vanilla extract - ½ teaspoon

Cooking directions:

1. Pour milk into a glass bowl that can be placed inside the slow cooker.
2. Add the chocolate, either as finely chopped or as a grated one into the glass bowl.
3. Place the bowl inside the slow cooker.
4. Pour water surrounding the bowl.
5. Cook it for 2 hours on low heat by stirring intermittently.
6. Once the chocolate is combined thoroughly with the milk, turn off the cooker and remove the glass bowl from the slow cooker.
7. Add vanilla extract and maple syrup to the bowl and stir well.
8. Spoon in the Greek yogurt in a large bowl and add the chocolate mixture on top of it.
9. Mix it well together before serving.
10. Refrigerate for two hours before serving.

Nutritional values:

Calories: 170 | Carbohydrate: 20.4g | Protein: 3.4g | Sugars: 17.9g | Fat: 8.3g | Dietary Fiber: 0.8g | Sodium: 42mg | Potassium: 130mg

8. Peanut Butter Banana Greek Yogurt Bowl

(Perfect Mediterranean Diet recipe)

Preparation: 5 minutes | Cooking: 2 hours | Servings: 4

Ingredients:

- Sliced bananas - 2
- Vanilla Greek yogurt - 4 cups
- Flaxseed meal - ¼ cup
- Creamy natural peanut butter - ¼ cup
- Nutmeg - 1 teaspoon

Cooking directions:

1. Divide the yogurt between four different bowls and top it with banana slices.
2. Add peanut butter into a small sized glass bowl and place in the slow cooker.
3. Pour water surrounding the glass bowl.
4. Under low heat setting, cook without covering the slow cooker until the peanut butter starts to melt.
5. The peanut butter should be in a thick consistency.
6. Once the butter turns to the required consistency, remove the bowl from the slow cooker.
7. Now, scoop one tablespoon of melted peanut butter and serve into the bowl with yogurt and bananas.
8. For each bowl, add about one tablespoon of melted peanut butter.
9. Sprinkle ground nutmeg and flax seed.

Nutritional values:

Calories: 187 | Carbohydrate: 19g | Protein: 6g | Sugars: 9g | Fat: 10.7g | Dietary Fiber: 4.5g | Sodium: 77mg | Potassium: 375mg

9. Italian Slow Cooker Banana Foster

Preparation time: 10 minutes | Cooking: 2 hours | Servings: 4

Ingredients:

- Bananas – 4
- Butter, melted – 4 tablespoons
- Rum - ¼ cup
- Brown sugar – 1 cup
- Cinnamon, ground - ½ teaspoon
- Vanilla extract – 1 teaspoon
- Coconut, shredded - ¼ cup
- Walnuts, chopped - ¼ cup

Instructions:

1. Peel the bananas, slice and keep ready to use.
2. Place the sliced bananas in the slow cooker in layers.
3. Mix the brown sugar, vanilla, butter, rum and cinnamon in a medium bowl thoroughly.
4. Pour the mix over the bananas.
5. Close the slow cooker and cook on low heat for 2 hours.
6. Sprinkle shredded coconut and walnuts on top before 30 of the end process.

Nutritional values:

Calories: 539 |Carbohydrates: 83.7g | Cholesterol: 31mg |Dietary Fiber: 4.7g | Protein: 3g | Potassium: 567mg | Sodium: 101mg| Sugars: 69g

10. Mediterranean Rice Pudding

Preparation: 10 minutes | Cooking: 2 hours | Servings: 8

Ingredients:

- Glutinous white rice, uncooked – 1 cup
- Evaporated milk – 12 ounces
- Cinnamon stick – 1 ounce
- White sugar – 1 cup
- Nutmeg, ground – 1 teaspoon
- Vanilla extract – 1 teaspoon

Instructions:

1. In a 6-quart slow cooker, put all the ingredients.

2. Cover the lid and cook on low heat for 1½ hours.
3. Stir intermittently, while cooking in progress.
4. Once ready, discard cinnamon stick and serve.

Nutritional values:

Calories: 321 | Carbohydrates: 56.4g |Cholesterol: 24mg |Dietary Fiber: 2.6g | Protein: 8.2g | Sodium: 102mg | Potassium: 322mg | Sugars: 35g

MEAL PLAN

7-Day Mediterranean Meal Plan

The 7 day Mediterranean meal plan envisages, the food has been cooking by people living in and around the Mediterranean Sea. In this meal plan, we have included recipes from Italy, Turkey, Morocco, Croatia, Spain, France, Greece, etc., as all these recipes can put in a larger canvass of Mediterranean food.

The recipes are one of the healthiest, using diverse spices and all are incredibly delicious to eat. The 7-day plan gives you an idea on how to manage a food style keeping to the Mediterranean tradition. The provided ingredients you can increase or decrease as per the serving demand.

The recipes have a wide variety which include some gluten-free, some vegetarian and including a wide selection of different meat and fish recipes. You can select your recipe wisely for a whole week from Monday to Sunday. Based on a 1500 calories per day plan, you can accomplish your fitness objective supported with exercise. You can easily shred 1-2 pounds weight in a week.

Monday

Breakfast – Slow Cooker Mediterranean Potatoes – 179.5 calories

Henry Wilson

Lunch – Slow Cooker Salmon Risotto - 320 calories
Dinner – Slow Cooker Mediterranean chicken - 278 calories

Tuesday

Breakfast – Slow Cooker Mediterranean Frittata - 164 calories
Lunch – Slow Cooker Chicken Posole - 105 calories
Dinner - Slow Cooker Greek Chicken - 399 calories

Wednesday

Breakfast – Crock Pot Mediterranean Rice & Vegetables - 271 calories
Lunch – Slow Cooker Chicken Parmesan Pasta – 455.5 calories
Dinner – Slow Cooker Seafood Stew - 215 calories

Thursday

Breakfast - Slow Cooker Spanish Chickpeas - 330 calories
Lunch - Slow Cooker Mediterranean Chicken Soup - 239 calories
Dinner - Crock Pot Mediterranean Chicken - 305 calories

Friday

Breakfast – Slow Cooker Ratatouille - 130 calories
Lunch – Slow Cooker Chicken & Vegetable Soup - 212 calories
Dinner - Slow Cooker Mediterranean Salmon - 225 calories

Saturday

Breakfast - Mediterranean Lentils and Rice - 98 calories

Lunch – Slow Cooker Mediterranean Pasta - 465 calories
Dinner - Crock Pot Italian Chicken – 388.6 calories

Sunday

Breakfast – Slow Cooker Spanish Rice - 55 calories
Lunch - Slow Cooker Pasta Meat Sauce with Ground Turkey - 201 calories
Dinner - Crock Pot Greek Chicken & Salad - 301 calories

Appetizers/Snacks:

Monday - Slow-Cooked Mediterranean Eggplant Salad - 67 calories
Tuesday - Peanut Butter Banana Greek Yogurt Bowl - 187 calories
Wednesday - Slow cooker Mediterranean Mushrooms - 60 calories
Thursday - Greek Yogurt Chocolate Mousse - 170 calories
Friday - Lentil, and chickpeas Appetizer - 251 calories
Saturday - Yam and Red bean Stew - 200 calories
Sunday - Crock Pot Mediterranean Chickpeas Stews - 178 calories

Conclusion

Thank you for reading this book. I hope you have understood exactly why you need to start a Mediterranean diet if you want to follow healthy eating. Whether you decide to adopt the philosophies of a Mediterranean diet fully or you want to take small steps, let this book be a foundation and inspiration to begin a new way of dieting. The great thing about adopting a Mediterranean diet is eating this way ensures your favorites foods are still available to you, in a healthier way.

When you follow the Mediterranean diet, the emphasis is on fresh, colorful eating with no heavily processed ingredients. Trust me; your plate will never be dull. And the better news is, though 'Diet' is in the name, it is a holistic approach to eating by including real foods as meals. Like any other typical diet, you won't be counting calories or Macronutrients in this. Let this book be an inspiration and guide for you to start with the Mediterranean diet and lead a healthy lifestyle.

Made in the USA
Middletown, DE
06 July 2019